penned in condominium world...
northwest florida's magnificent
emerald coast

Fun and Adventure in the

Condo

Lifestyle

owners, board members, managers
...learn how to better manage and
maintain your condominium

James Keir Baughman

2003

ISBN 9780979044328

CONTENTS

Dedication

The "gut burning" urge to write is ofttimes a puzzling, compelling emotion. To be sure, even we who suffer may not fully comprehend it's siren call. Still, millions share that whispering inner insistence, and the writing itself might convey a sense of purpose for a while.

Writers are simply people who seem especially attuned to some vibrant experience, or agony, or event seeming so momentous - at least to us - that it must be recorded, invoked, enduring, never fading into a dusty attic of the lost.

And yet, the penned word will have meaning only to one, until another happens along...an editor or publisher who mutters quietly at an office desk..."gee, this guy (or gal) can write. And look!... he (or she) may even have some grasp of what we're trying to accomplish."

That's why this book is dedicated to Lisa Pinder of Fort Lauderdale, Florida. Lisa is a youthful, vivacious, inordinately effective, journalism executive who juggles two vital careers. One is a home, husband, and children she obviously cherishes. The other is as the Editor of "Managers Report."

You'll have guessed by now..., she is that special editor...the one who gave this writer the chance to be published, to learn the value of a great editor's considerate guidance, to grow as a writer, to be circulated again and again, to reach even the heady attainment of penning feature and cover articles.

To fully fathom it, one should know the vital niche her company's magazine "Managers Report" has attained in it's vastly growing industry. You see "Managers Report" has long been the pre-eminent "self help" and "how to" national magazine for those who lead America's community associations.

Like others in it's field, the publication certainly reports effectively on the social side of community association living.

But far better than the others, it shares a world of insight involving community association management problems and how to solve them..., to direct more effectively, improve finances, have board members work together more efficiently, augment

security, fortify building maintenance, beautify landscaping...,
hire, train, and keep more efficient employees.

Launched by her father Ivor Thomas, wisely groomed and
expanded over many years,"Managers Report," at Ivor's retirement, is now owned by a publishing company.

Because of her success, though, Lisa Pinder has stayed on
board as editor and led the magazine through exciting changes,
a major new look for the cover, and an up-to-the-minute edito-
rial content revision.

"Managers Report," and Lisa Pinder's craft, reach the desk
of thousands of condo managers every month and a great many
community association officers and board members. Likely, if
every board studied it's pages from cover to cover managing
would go much more smoothly all across America.

Even more, though, when every condo owner has a subscription to "Managers Report," and reads it judicially, there will be
far greater understanding, wiser leadership, more cooperation,
and greater ease in managing condominiums and other community associations successfully.

You can find out how to get a subscription on the internet by
clicking on www.managersreport.com. Or you may write to
Advantage Publishing Co., Inc, 100 Nix Road, Little Rock AR
72211 or simply call 1-800-425-1314

About The Author

THE AUTHOR was born in Richmond, of an old Virginia family. Fourteen growing years were spent on a 60 acre family farm in it's rural suburb, Varina.

The Indian maiden, Pocohontas lived in Varina with her pioneer husband John Rolfe in the earliest years of our nation. It is also the community where Thomas Jefferson's daughter Martha lived with her husband, Thomas Mann Randolph, Jr on his 950 acre plantation. Many Civil War battles were fought in and near Varina, and the author's grandfather, James Wilson Baughman, built the main house inside a Civil War fort which remained on the farm.

After World War II, the author lived in Rome, Georgia, then Birmingham, Alabama. During four high school years he served in the Alabama educational systems Army Reserve Officer Training Corps and the Alabama Air National Guard. .

In July of 1949, on a two week military sojourn, James Keir Baughman found Northwest Florida's magnificent Emerald Coast. In that same year his family bought acreage at Miramar Beach in South Walton County, just east of Fort Walton Beach.

On June 1st, 1951 his parents Elba A. and Iris Keir Armour Baughman invested in a small conglomerate of retail businesses in Shalimar, a suburb of Fort Walton Beach, and moved the family there.

The author began writing as an ad copywriter, columnist, news writer, and advertising manager at Fort Walton Beach's weekly Playground News in 1956. During an extensive career in business management, marketing, and advertising he published thousands of lines of copy as an advertising copywriter. In retirement he has written for national and regional magazines of the condo management and sailing genre.

He served 10 ½ years as a Fort Walton Beach City Councilman, one year as Mayor Pro Tempore.

Over the years, he served on Boards of Directors for the JayCees, Northwest Florida Regional Planning Council, Playground Area Safety Council, YMCA, Fort Walton Yacht Club,

Holy Trinity Lutheran Church, Greater Fort Walton Beach Chamber of Commerce, Fort Walton Beach Downtown Merchants Assn, as a management advisor for Junior Achievement, as a Lieutenant in the Navarre Squadron of the Civil Air Patrol, was active in the Florida League of Cities, Rotary Club, and Lions Club.

His mother Iris Keir Armour Baughman guided the Greater Fort Walton Beach Chamber of Commerce for 14 years as Executive Director. He and his family members have owned ten business enterprises over the 52 year span.

The pinnacle of his business career, prior to retirement, was as a Florida Licensed Community Association Manager, managing two 7 story hi-rises in Destin. In earlier years he was a residential and rental condo owner and board member.

The author's love of sailing began five decades ago when he found Northwest Florida's emerald hued waters. He and his wife Sandee live along side the Gulf Coast Intra-Coastal Waterway reaching 800 miles through five states to the Mexican border.

His children: James and wife Diane, Jill, Dana and husband Brent, are all Fort Walton Beach and Destin professionals or business owners who pursue his enchantment with the delightful Emerald Coast lifestyle. His granddaughter Mary Grace joined the family on March 30, 2003.

Introduction

Some of these helpful essays have already been published....once...in national and regional professional magazines.

For the scribe, being published is a wondrous thing. But, with specialized, informative writing, being published only once may be a decided dilemma.

Why? Well each of these tales was willfully crafted to share new ways of solving difficulties that bedevil those of us who are owners, leaders, or managers in our condo and community associations.

The month in which a magazine is published articles, and the lessons they describe, likely have high visibility, many readers. But then, when the following month's issue comes out, all the wisdom of the month before fades into long ago, to dusty, unseen files, quickly hidden, forgotten.

Truth is, though, much of the wisdom in these articles is genuinely timeless, bearing tips and new ideas that may continue to help make many of us better leaders and managers of our condominium environment.

So..., why not select those the writer deems most useful, gather them together in one place...like a book...that cannot so easily fade into last month's long ago...?

Ta-Daaaaaa...!!! That's just what we've done!

All the following articles, crafted, some published, in the past three or four years seem to a great extent, ageless in context of the community association quandaries they point out, solutions they discover.

To be sure, though, the insight, the answers are not all of the author himself. What you may learn in these pages comes from people just like you, condo and community association owners, board members, officers, managers... all across America.

They've been kind enough to subject themselves and their fellow association members to interview, to tell their tales of problem and successful accomplishment in the intense spotlight of national publication. It's often a bit scary to most folk, but what a way to serve your fellow man...or woman!

You'll find far more, though, than just dilemma and resolution in these pages.

There's fun, too... word pictures of owners, board members, association officers, managers much like yourself. People who've made a difference in a lifestyle similar to yours. And too, there are word pictures of places in America you might not have yet seen, visions of condos or community associations that might be quite different from yours.

Mostly, perhaps, there are reminders of why you chose the condo or community association lifestyle...encouragement that it can be made even better...hints as to how to skirt the major stumbling blocks to fruitful living, and effective management.

There's just one caution. Even with passage of time, in human context, many things stay the same. But some change. So, remember to apply these ideas in the broader sense, fine tuning them to fit your own time, your own particular community association, your own members, your own special part of America, especially the current laws of your own State or City, or County. If you do those things effectively and well...how can you miss?

JAMES KEIR BAUGHMAN

Fun and Adventure in the

Condo

Lifestyle

High Mountain Weather...
Charm and Challenge

To understand either, is to know the ambience which gives life to Mountain Spirit. Take it from one who's been there. Broad, placid Moreno Valley, 8,400 feet high in northern New Mexico's rugged Sangre de Christo mountains is one of America's most beautiful spots. At it's southern end, where the foothills of the Sangre de Christos stretch out like a drowsy, lumpy giant in a Laz-E-Boy, every craggy hill looks down into another lush, green mini-valley...each one a natural, God-given summer pasture feeding 30 or 40 fat, sleek reddish-brown cattle.

Moreno Valley's Angel Fire seems just as sleepy in it's summer passage, a wee mountain village just biding the time 'til winter snowfall and the rush of ski season. Close by, Angel Fire Resort clings to the foothills. The abutting cluster of individually owned condominiums that greatly expand it's ski accommodations actually climb a ways up the slopes, into the mountain Pinon and Aspen forest, but not nearly so far as the 2,000 feet it takes to ride on up to the top of the ski lift.

45 unit, Mountain Spirit Condominium, is one of those closest to Angel Fire Resort, in fact just across the parking lot. "If you think summer is nice," says Jeff Dahl, six year owner and board member, and five year president of Mountain Spirit Homeowner Association, "you ought to see these mountains in October when the Aspen leaves turn fiery gold."

Angel Fire, though, was born many, many moons ago when Indians came back to their villages with tales of flaming red sunrises and sunsets, glows which seemed to turn hoarfrost in the trees and mountain snow and mist into "fires of the gods...."

"Actually," Dahl expounds, "we're truly a four season resort area." In late spring, summer, and early fall, Angel Fire has great golf, tennis, hiking, and horseback riding on mountain trails, as well as fly fishing for trout in Eagle Lake, Monte Verde Lake, and mountain streams. There's sailing on the lakes, too. And for a great view of the Moreno Valley, summer visitors can ride to the top of the ski lift.

"For a high mountain town," Dahl adds, "Angel Fire has one of the best airports around." The tallest mountains are on each side so aircraft final approaches and departures are over miles of flat valley with just low foothills far away at each end. The 9,000 foot paved runway allows access to Angel Fire even by fast corporate jets.

"In the fall," Dahl continues, "a lot of people come to see the leaves change color, and others just love to see spring come to the mountains." At the 8,400 foot altitude, summer daytime temperatures range from the mid 70's to the low 80's, with nights in the high 50's to low 60's. In April, October, and November days reach only 60 degrees or so and nights will be a bit below freezing, in the 25 to 30 degree range.

Angel Fire's big season, it's long season, though, is ski time. "Angel Fire is the second largest ski area in New Mexico," Dahl says. "Starting in late October we have snow on the ground almost continuously until mid April or so, but the ski season runs from Thanksgiving to late March." Daytime temperatures in winter are usually well below freezing, averaging 10 to 15 degrees. Nights normally hover near zero, often below. Angel Fire's sister town, Eagle Nest, 7 miles north in the Moreno Valley holds the record for the lowest temperature ever recorded in New Mexico, 35 degrees below zero.

"Of course, the long winter season, the high altitude, and the cold bring us a lot of snow, and that's great for our ski business," Dahl adds, "but those same things bring Mountain Spirit homeowners significant maintenance problems that are quite different from some found at lower altitudes." Insurance coverage remains basic, however, according to Dahl. In other words there's no special cold or snow insurance necessary that compare to the flood and windstorm insurance costs faced by Southern oceanfront community associations.

Needless to say, though, snow removal is a recurring cost, an item in every year's planning. "We budget $500 for snow removal by truck," Dahl explains, "and another $500 for hand shoveling." That cost could be far more except that Mountain Spirit Condominium has underground parking protected from snow pileup.

Also favorable is that Mountain Spirit lies close by Angel Fire Resort and near the highway, so the entrance drive area that must be cleared of snow is mercifully short.

Firewood is another vital budget consideration. Every home in the 45 unit condo has at least one fireplace. Many have two. In an area of small, far-outlying communities with winter temperatures often well below zero, the risk of electric power loss is not a thing to face without a dependable alternate source of heat. We can't remember seeing any, not one, of the outlying homes and chalets or condos without a fireplace chimney. Since all but two of Mountain Spirit's homes are rental units, the provision of firewood and the maintenance of fireplaces and chimneys is an ongoing expense. And, of course, heating and electricity costs during the long winter are substantial budget considerations.

"But, probably the toughest maintenance problem we have to confront," says Dahl, "is ice." At such high altitude temperatures are not only very cold, they drop quickly. When the thermometer eases above freezing, rain may fall instead of snow. On a sunny day some snow melts. Then, like anywhere else, water finds even the tiniest cracks in which to hide. "At high altitudes," Dahl explains, "just a few hours later it's near zero again and the water expands into hard, swelling, unyielding ice." With this process occurring over and over again, tiny cracks in the roof and around chimneys are pried open and become leaks or buckled roofing surfaces. Cracks in the entrance drive paving become potholes, and in the same way the ice attacks siding walls, balconies, wooden railings, even concrete. Dahl's description reminded this writer of the pervasive salt air corrosion that comparatively invades oceanfront condominium properties.

"Presently we're in the planning stage to refurbish the entire roof on the Mountain Spirit complex because we've had a continuing problem with leaks," Dahl said. "In the initial engineering study it looks like we're going to have to replace every panel of the roof decking." Adding even more expense, the Mountain Spirit board of directors felt the problem serious enough to warrant paying for a complete inspection of all underlying roof joists and beams. "We were really relieved that those proved to be still in good shape," Dahl added.

Planning for re-roofing has been the board of director's largest major project in the current electoral term. The approximately $100,000 expense will come from budgeted reserves. Mountain

Spirit's new roof surface will be of galvanized steel, pre-coated to further extend the metal's life. The weather coating, as is the present one, will be an earth tone that enhances the natural pine siding of the building.

"A major structural difference brought about by the high mountain climate," Dahl further explains, "is that the steel roofing sections are installed with screws instead of nails...thousands and thousands of them." Sealing the sections down tightly with screws lessens openings where water can hide, freeze, and expand...forcing apart and damaging roof sections. It also strengthens roof panels against high wind gusts, common to the mountain region. Needless to say, that process is more costly because it is time consuming, far more labor intensive than using a nail gun.

Another factor adding to the cost, and continuing maintenance, of Mountain Spirit's roof is the need for careful sealing of 45 chimneys. "If ice gets in the caulking around the chimneys it's an instant leak, Dahl says, "so it has to be done meticulously." Luckily, in the original design, multiple fireplaces at Mountain Spirit were channeled into one chimney per unit. "If not," Dahl says, "we'd have more than twice as many problem areas."

Jeffrey A. Dahl is an attorney, specializing in commercial litigation. He and his family live in Albuquerque, 150 or so miles south of Angel Fire. So he's able to visit frequently to inspect the condominium and to consult with Jimmy Linton, property manager for Angel Fire Resort Management Services which oversees the property.

"In a small way, we have a special claim to fame," he says, "one we're rather proud of." Mountain Spirit is one of thousands of properties taken over by the Resolution Trust Corporation, the private federal government agency established to recover billions of dollars for taxpayers when junk bonds and failed real estate investments forced so many Savings and Loans into bankruptcy.

"At the time, I was serving as the attorney for Angel Fire Resort, so we knew almost immediately when the S&L that owned Mountain Spirit was in trouble." Dahl and other area New Mexico business leaders believed that local ownership and management could do a better job, setting up a real estate investment partnership, Moreno Valley, Inc.

4

"As soon as the RTC was ready to release Mountain Spirit, we made them an offer and finally worked out a deal we felt was favorable to everyone."

Dahl and his New Mexican partners inherited problems, of course. Nearly half of the 45 units were still sitting there unsold. Working together with local management they brought the property back up to standard and sold out all of the remaining units. Now Mountain Spirit is far more than just a source of enjoyment for it's owners. It has become a valuable force in the economic success of New Mexico's Angel Fire and the Moreno Valley.

"A lot of people," says Jeff Dahl, "thought the RTC would never work, or worse, that it would take a couple of decades to recover lost tax dollars. Mountain Spirit, today, is a tribute to the RTC's success, to a good working relationship between government and free enterprise."

Superior Maintenance
Boosts Property Values

"The list of our members who believe a continuing, effective maintenance program is the key to sustaining peak property values goes back 30 years to our first board of directors," says John J. "Jack" Herring, year 2000 president of El Matador Condominium.

"Moreover," Herring elaborates, "we've long been convinced that efficient building, mechanical, and landscape preservation creates the basis for quality of life in the family-like proximity of community association living."

Jack Herring should know. He remains an original unit owner of the first high-rise condominium built in the Fort Walton Beach/Destin area, the heart of Northwest Florida's Emerald Coast.

"El Matador's charter was signed in 1970," Jack says. "We first took occupancy in 1971, with the homeowners assuming full control of the association on January 1, 1977."

El Matador is an ocean front, barrier island, community, located directly on Gulf of Mexico beaches, famous for the whitest sand in the world.

"Truth is," Herring expounds, "we're surrounded by the best water views imaginable." Ocean vistas stretch to the south horizon. A stones throw across waterfront homes along Santa Rosa Boulevard lies Santa Rosa Sound, the tugboat and yacht-busy intra-coastal waterway. "From El Matador east," Jack says, "our Gulf beaches stretch for 14 miles in pristine, natural state, totally undeveloped, because they're on U. S. Air Force property.

An avid angler, Herring often fishes in the surf along El Matador beaches catching Pompano and Whiting. "I caught three this morning," he says during our interview, "and I already had several in the freezer."

There's far more of tropical, Spanish flavor to the surroundings of El Matador than it's dashing toreador name. Orange-red tile roofs add a sense of opulence found less often in today's tight-budget construction designs, and a wealth of tall palm trees add a landscape lushness usually enjoyed only in southern Florida.

"In fact the palms, themselves, are an indication of management efficiency," Herring says. Palm trees, not indigenous to the area, must be transplanted from more central parts of the state, carefully maintained, and occasionally replaced.

"Our 300,000 square feet of lawn grass at El Matador," Herring explains, "is highly unusual in condos today because of land cost. And we truly enjoy it." Set in the wide expanse of green lawn and palm trees, El Matador's five main buildings tower six stories, each comprising 10 one bedroom and 50 two bedroom units. A sixth building houses 16 efficiency units. Amenities include two large swimming pools - heated in winter, 2 tennis courts, 2 whirlpools, 2 saunas, and an exercise room. Association gatherings are held in an expansive, beautifully appointed meeting room surrounded by glass walls that overlook greenery of the landscape.

Reasonable maintenance fees cover costs for a number of individual unit expenses including water, sewage, trash removal, cable television, gated security, lawn and landscape maintenance, and pest control.

"Activities make El Matador a special place," Jacks relates. In fact, his wife Marti Herring has long chaired El Matador's Social Committee, the most active on the Island. Guests and residents participate in weekly bridge and domino games, croquet, bingo, free movies, and a weekly happy hour. Several parties have become major annual events. There are celebrations for New Year's, Halloween, Valentine's Day, St. Patrick's Day, Thanksgiving, and Superbowl Sunday, as well as impromptu activities such as pool parties, fishing trips, shopping sprees, and group tours to nearby casinos on the Mississippi coast.

"After thirty years, El Matador is in beautiful condition," Jack says, "and so far we've haven't had need of a major concrete restoration." Herring and his fellow board members point to three basic requirements for maintenance success.

"First of all," says Jack, "a detailed, continuing maintenance program was set up by our first boards, and other association officers have followed it religiously over the years." El Matador's buildings are re-sealed and painted, throughout, every five years. Many, if not most, associations choose a ten year maintenance schedule. "We do one of the five major buildings each year," Herring says. A daily or monthly maintenance schedule is followed for all mechanical equipment, as well as pools, elevators, and the like. "For instance," Jack counts, "El Matador has 38 pumps that move water."

Second, according to Herring, is the importance of well funded maintenance reserves. A sound program of monthly assessments for funding maintenance reserve accounts was set up by early El Matador boards, has always been followed to the letter, and recalculated as inflation increased the costs of repair. "Because of the wise leadership of early boards," says Herring, and because we've closely followed their lead, we've always had ample funding to do the vital preventative maintenance that's needed." In fact, more than 26% of El Matador's monthly assessments are banked for preservation and replacement reserves.

Third, says Herring, is the good fortune to have a design, construction methods, and materials that were originally conceived with long life and ease of continuing maintenance in mind. "Few hi-rise condos today," he remarks, "are built like the El Matador." For instance, El Matador's exterior surfaces are not bearing walls, but of concrete block construction, not dependant on decayable interior steel re-bar. Steel reinforcing is limited only to the building's support columns and floor slabs, making inspection and repair of spalling much more contained and focused. Another design aspect that has facilitated concrete maintenance at El Matador is that balconies and walkways are not cantilevered, but strongly supported by steel reinforced columns. "We feel that reduced stress on concrete and steel components seems to extend the life of balconies and walkways," Jack reports. "And let's not forget," Herring adds, "that all of our boards have been relentless in seeking the best concrete repair contractors, checking and double-checking, and fully repairing even the smallest early sign of spalling.

"We certainly don't overlook the fact that, even with the best maintenance program, age creeps up on you," Jack remarks. In fact, it's virtually impossible for a bidding contractor to fully anticipate the results of a spalling inspection check. Herring and fellow board members got an unsettling surprise last year when one building's five year resealing, painting, and concrete repair costs soared 70% over budget. "Of course," Jack says, "that means an astute board should recalculate reserve funding to fully meet, obviously more realistic needs."

Another basic philosophy that has contributed greatly to El Matador's success has been an on-going effort to retain employees on a long term basis. "We think of ourselves as a family at El Matador," Jack says, "and that especially includes our employees." John Wright has been El Matador's licensed community association manager for more than five years. But for the prior fifteen years, he excelled as Maintenance Supervisor. His 17 person staff, surprisingly small for such expansive acreage and 366 units, includes Cindy Gaspie as Office Administrator, Wanda Ward as Bookkeeper, and Harry Crawford who supervises housekeeping staff and security personnel. A number of employees have been with El Matador for five to ten years.

Jack and Marti Herring were rental owners at El Matador for many years while he pursued his career as a naval aviator and civil service flight instructor training military pilots. However, during those busy years he still found time to serve on a number of El Matador committees, traveling from their home in Memphis.

The first two years after retirement were spent directing a complete renovation of their condominium unit. Becoming active again in association leadership Herring served on several key committees including Building & Grounds, Personnel, Property Management, and Budget & Finance, before accepting a two year election to El Matador's board of directors. Board members cannot be elected for a third consecutive year, but may serve again after a one year hiatus. "Our term limitation may be a bit unusual," Jack says, "but we think it has served us well in assuring owners that no self-serving group is controlling the board for long periods of time. It also helps board members to set aside politics and focus on good management."

"Serving as president of such a large association can be a tough job," says John White, El Matador's CAM Manager, "but with 30 years of experience as rental owner, resident, chairman of vital committees, and two years as a board member, Jack Herring is ideal as El Matador's president."

Herring, himself, is quick to point out that his leadership follows a pattern set by many other owners, association officers, committee activists, managers, and loyal, capable employees who have brought the condominium community to it's present state of excellence. There is understandable pride, though, when Herring also points out for all the El Matador "family" that success is in the numbers. El Matador property values, in the year 2003, are more than nine times the unit purchase price in 1970.

THE BAREFOOT STREETS OF. . .
SAN PEDRO TOWN

Sunrise is magnificent. Even if morning is not your friend, you'll come to the edge of the lagoon to watch stars and sea-black night fade into the Caribbean dawn. Landlubbers know sunrise as a thing of the eastern sky. On the islands it is a happening of the ocean itself. A pink froth on clouds far out to sea whispers of the coming sun, until pale rose watercolors the crystal blue of morning. When dawn finds San Pedro Town, the world seems hushed, looking into the sea breeze, waiting breathlessly for a sliver of fire on the ocean's rim. The glowing star that lights our lives climbs up from the bowels of the sea, bearing the gift of a new day and tropic heat that makes Belizeans easy, relaxed, slow moving in their ways.

San Pedro Town is on the island of Ambergris Caye, a living part of the second longest barrier reef in the world, the largest in the Americas. Only the Great Barrier Reef of Australia is longer.

It is the only town on Belizean reef islands that range for 185 miles along the Caribbean coast of the Central American country. Like Belize itself, the 2,000 inhabitants of San Pedro Town are unhurried, a world apart from the honking, bustling concrete canyons and condos of America's cities. Residents and visitors on the 27 mile spit of earth and coral live amid unspoiled natural beauty of ocean and reef, lagoon, a broad bay that makes mainland a faraway place, soft sand of shore, the breezy shade of palm trees.

Belizeans are fiercely protective of their way of life, of the ecology and Mayan history of their land. They don't want another glitzy Cancun in their backyard to rob them of a peaceful pace or the grandeur of nature and their proud past.

So the focus of those who come to share San Pedro Town and the reef islands will be genuine relaxation ...a sense that time has stopped, that television is not a compelling affair, a deep

11

awareness of the warmth of the sun and salty tang of sea winds. Living is so casual that neckties are forbidden at some resorts. You'll never find a native wearing one.

The streets of San Pedro Town are of nothing but white sand making bare feet the Nikes of the island. You'll still find a few thatched roofs as on the South Pacific islands of Bali or Tahiti. There are no cars. Transportation is no a big deal, anyway. Everything - restaurants, gift shops, island saloons, fishing, reef diving, fun - is within walking distance of lodging and the sea. Local land and water taxis can be had for a price, but most who prefer not to walk rent a golf cart.

This barefoot way of life is just a couple of hours away from Houston, New Orleans, and Miami. American or Continental Airlines jet to Belize, as does Taca, the Airline of El Salvador, which serves much of Latin America with modern Boeing 737 and 757 jet liners.

San Pedro Town is a seventeen minute flight from the mainland by Air Belize, Island Air, Tropic Air, and Maya Airways, but you can cross the bay by boat if a slower pace suits you. It's a nice trip. And it's nice to find there's no jostling by impatient crowds.

In addition to the 2,000 who call it home, there are only about 50 resort and mini-condo lodgings, totaling 730 or so guest rooms in San Pedro Town. Many are small, some with as few as three to five units. If you don't live there, reservations are important. A free phone call to the U.S. office of the Belize Tourist Board brings all the information needed. Americans and Canadians are required to have only a passport to enter the country.

With such promises of tranquillity and seclusion, the hint of somnolence and ease, what can the visitor expect for fun? Well, the larger resorts have swimming pools and swim-up bars, jacuzzis, and tennis courts, a few lighted for night play. Larger, by the way, means 60 or 70 guest units. And there's volley ball, basketball, table games, play areas for kids, barbeque grilles. Don't forget the surrounding sea for boating, sailing, and fishing. There's always sunbathing on the shore of the lagoon. A family picnic in the shade of a windswept palm tree appeals to many who live there.

Still, it's the undersea fantasy world of the barrier reef that is the pride of island Belizeans and brings many who love coastal living to the sleepy peacefulness of San Pedro Town.

Surface snorkeling is a simple way to experience it. The less bold just peer from the boat into the blaze of color and sea creatures, the society of the reef. The sea is so clear you can see for twenty or thirty feet down.

Scuba diving, though, is the best way to share it, eyeball to eyeball with thousands of brightly colored fish. There are a number of qualified scuba service shops and boat tours available. In fact, San Pedro Town and the reef have long been the secret hideaway of knowledgeable Scuba divers in the Americas. The northern end of the reef begins at Ambergris Caye and forms the quiet lagoon which protects San Pedro Town's shore from Caribbean waves.

For a barefoot town, there's still enough nightlife and good seafood to put a kick in the existence of San Pedranos. Visitors join in with a "Yo-ho-ho!" and the bottle of rum expected in the Caribbean, but there are exotic tropical cocktails and even vintage wines in the Caribbean Trader Bar at Journey's End Resort. On many a night there'll be dancing to steel band rhythms at Jerry Gilbreath's Purple Parrot Bar.

Ramon Nunez will point the way toward the great restaurant at Ramon's Village Resort in San Pedro Town. But, you may find Richard Headrick on one of his frequent inspections. Richard is the Mississippi entrepreneur who consummated his love of Latin America when he acquired Ramon's in the mid 80's. Through his talent and business skill Ramon's thatch roofed lodgings have become one of the most captivating little resorts in Central America overlooking the lagoon, the barrier reef, and the Caribbean Sea.

It's simply another world, far different from the high rise condo's we talk about in most of these articles. It's a world you might love to share come vacation time... the far away feel, the nearby, discrete ambience of a serene South Pacific hide-away.

ABUSIVE NEIGHBORS ...

A GROWING HAZARD TO CONDOMINIUM LIVING

It happened in a high rise condominium on peaceful Holiday Isle, an upscale spit of land separating Northwest Florida's Destin harbor from emerald waters of the Gulf of Mexico. Sadly, not once..., but twice. Agitated, malicious male home owners cornered the middle-aged manager, a lady by-the-way, against the wall of her office, screaming in her face until she was in tears.

Worse, these...uhhh...gentlemen, who completely demolished the bounds of decency and business decorum (not to mention common courtesy toward women) were present or past board members of the condo association.

Sadly, such abuse is common in the condo world. It is a national problem, far from limited to the beautiful beaches of Northwest Florida. To be fair, it is defined by a very small percentage of owners who somehow feel their partial ownership of the larger condo property gives them an unbounded right to use strident aggression and belligerence to get their way. Even though they are a very few, the viciousness of their conduct sharply magnifies it's effect.

Managers are deeply discouraged by such abuse, which severely hinders their management effectiveness. Far too many, often the most capable, simply abandon the industry. After all, good managers can easily find career slots that provide a supportive, effective environment. As a result damage to the management of condominium associations is wide spread, though functionally hidden in a welter of association politics and state legislation that pretends to allow the "freedom" of each owner to "control" his or her own "home" just as though it were a singly owned property. At the same time, there is total failure in safeguarding professional management's ability to manage effectively for the far greater majority of owners.

Sam Dolnick of La Mesa, California, who served as president of his association for seven years puts it squarely in perspective. "Of course", he says, "the board and manager must minimize frustrations by being open and responsive to the needs of all homeowners. But we all know", he continues, "that there are 2% or so of owners in many associations who are truly abusive and selfish in their relationships with manager, board, and other owners".

Rick Cummings, general manager of The Waterford Condominiums in Kensington, Maryland agrees. "A lot of people in our industry now say that the abusive owner is the one remaining barrier to good management. Not only do we lose managers, but often the most capable owners won't run for the board because of the abuse they have to take. In many cases association members just get fed up and sell their units because of the abusive behavior of a few fellow owners".

As a licensed professional manager, I've learned that abuse of the manager or board is abuse of the corporate structure, the "chain of command." It can be as damaging to the association as physical assault, a very real danger to property and finances. After all, management's greatest successes are found in a positive work environment based on cooperation and encouragement which protects the rights and property values for everyone.

Jerry Fien, long term president of the Woodlands Condominium in West Orange New Jersey says it best, "when a strong president and stable board support a good manager, the interference and stress caused by a few abusive owners can be minimized or endured" .

It is when abusive owners display enough power, or generate enough fear, to divide or paralyze the board of directors that the most severe risks befall the property and the organization. I've seen such selfish, aggressive people hog storage space, grant each other special favors, increase building decay through lack of maintenance, undermine the rental program, increase insurance risks through poor safety control, ineffectively manage capital reserves, even to providing an atmosphere conducive to embezzlement of association funds.

Sam Dolnick, says it even more clearly, "abusive owners are driven by their own narrow interests, not the realistic needs of the association". To further illustrate this point, in my own experience in Northwest Florida, I found that managers before me improperly used association funds to pay for repairs inside private units. They failed to pursue legal steps to determine proper liability because they were afraid to confront powerful, abusive owners in the community association.

In that same Northwest Florida association, a small group of abusive owners fired four managers in six years, with the association constantly in turmoil. They regained control of their board and fired the fourth manager just after Hurricane Opal caused severe damage to the condominium. After ignoring the manager's warnings, they failed to replace the roof in time, and let rainwater wreck more than 100 units left undamaged by the storm.

In another association, three of five members of the board of directors met secretly... to pre-decide board action and lost a multi-million dollar lawsuit because of ill-advised settlement.

"Over the past ten years", says Ellen Hirsch de Haan, a St. Petersburg, Florida attorney who specializes in community association law, "I've noticed a sharp increase in the number of abusive owners. Ten years ago it was rare to attend a meeting in which there was loud, angry disorder. Today it is commonplace, and it's no longer just the manager and board members who face the abuse. As the association attorney, abusive owners have spit on me, screamed right in my face, threatened, and cursed me with the foulest of language. Many owners who would make the best board members just won't serve anymore".

Abusive owners put other owners at risk when they insult rental guests over use of the pool; endanger the building by refusing to place condo keys in the emergency key bank; disagree with law, documents, or board policy and vent anger by yelling at employees; force their own interpretation of law and documents at meetings; act as self-appointed policemen, push to increase unnecessary self-serving "rules"; enter locked common areas or files without authorization; threaten and criticize every manager.

What is an abusive owner? Psychologists separate damaging human interaction into three broad categories: physical, sexual, and emotional abuse. Physical and sexual abuse are criminal acts and should be handled by law enforcement authorities.

However, those interviewed say abuse confronted in community management is usually emotional. Yelling, cursing, foul language, and threats are common threads. Wider damage is caused by the abusive owner's tenacity to control... refusing to honor corporate structure set by law to protect the rights of all owners. They wield criticism, harassment, voting manipulation, and belligerence toward management staffers to bully their personal desires.

Dr. Harvey L. Ruben, M.D., professor of clinical psychiatry at Yale Medical School says, "abusive personalities can be found in any group of people, but a bit of power such as condo ownership is likely to intensify their drive to control. They play by different rules from the rest of us. Everything has to be done their way and they have little sense of courtesy or feelings for others. Some are 'Type A' personalities, time urgent, hostile, competitive. Some are emotionally ill. Some are sociopaths without conscience toward others, totally self-centered and self absorbed. With them winning is everything and anything goes, so the end justifies the means. With all of these abusive people the traits get even more intense as they get older".

" Frankly", Dr. Ruben continues, " there is no good way to deal with these abusive personalities except through laws and penalties to control abusive behavior."

Since regulation and professional management have brought us far toward control of most other community association problems, what can sensible board members and managers do to help tear down this last barrier to effective association management?

"First of all", says Peter S. Philbin, an attorney with the firm of Rees, Broome & Diaz of Vienna, Virginia, "the board must establish meeting procedures which balance the right of every owner to speak, with the need of the board to do it's work. A homeowner has the right to attend and observe a board meeting, but not the right to interject or interfere in board discussions or voting. An open forum for questions or discussions from the audience should be scheduled at the beginning or end of the board meeting. The chairman must have the courage to gavel an abuser out of order, to adjourn the meeting if interference becomes a problem, or to legally remove disruptive persons if necessary.

"Then", Philbin continues, "the board must establish rules for management to follow in dealing with abusive behavior or interference. The wise manager will have these procedures written into the employment contract. The manager should be required to respond to abusive talk or interference by ending the conversation and telling the abuser that the complaint must be sent to the board in writing".

All of those interviewed agreed that there are other things that sincere board members and managers must try in dealing with abusive people, although there is no guarantee of success. Openness and responsiveness to all owners is vital. Be a good listener and take care of problems quickly. Keep your sense of humor and use patience, kindness, and professionalism in dealing with everyone, especially those who choose to be hostile. Try to elicit the help of a critical owner by putting him or her on a committee. Ask the abuser's friends, if he or she has any, to help solve the problem. Remain as calm and objective as possible in the face of abuse.

Rick Cummings, as with most homeowners and professionals interviewed, goes further, "legislation is needed", he says, "to shield association management from abuse and interference and to provide a judicial review system with penalties for those determined to abuse or interfere".

John Dyckmans, a community association homeowner of Pocono Summit, Pennsylvania agrees. "I've seen board members just resign in disgust and often the best ones won't run anymore. We need laws that prevent this kind of abuse from affecting management ".

Personally, this writer/ex-manager believes that legislation should require a manager to report abuse or damaging interference to state regulators. A committee composed of the association attorney, manager, and two directors should investigate and report to regulators or the courts for further enforcement action. They should be required to complete the review even if summarily fired. "After all", says attorney Ellen Hirsch de Haan, "the last resort to end such abuse and protect the properties of reasonable owners is legislation and the courts".

10 Tips For Dealing
With Abusive Owners

TIP 1.
Be open and responsive to all homeowner requests and complaints.

TIP 2.
Be a good listener. Quickly provide answers in writing and take care of problems immediately.

TIP 3.
Deal with every owner, even hostile ones, with patience, kindness, and professionalism. Keep your sense of humor. Remember the 98% of owners who make your job easy.

TIP 4.
If abuse is caused by criticism of one management area suggest that the disgruntled owner serve on a committee to study the problem.

TIP 5.
Enlist the help of friends of the abusive owner to find out why he or she is so dissatisfied and help you work toward a better understanding and relationship.

TIP 6.

Set meeting rules to balance the right of owners to speak, with the need of the board to do its work. A board meeting is to conduct association business, not to argue owner gripes.

TIP 7.

Have courage to gavel abusive attendees out of order, adjourn the meeting if interference is a problem, and legally remove uncontrollable persons.

TIP 8.

Have a written agreement as to how the board and manager will work together to handle abuse, harassment, or interference. The wise manager has this in the employment contract.

TIP 9.

Remain calm and objective. Remember that people who are the most damaging to those around them are often suffering from personality or emotional disorders.

TIP 10.

Urge your community association members to push for legislation to control abuse, harassment, and interference in the association management process.

LIKE CONDOS, FAMILIES ARE THE
HEART OF THIS ASSOCIATION, TOO!

"We have a lot of husband and wife crews in Catalina 22 racing," says Pam Slaton of Gainesville, Georgia. "It seems to me that families are the driving force, the heart, of Catalina 22 sailing competition."

Pam and her husband Dennis have been sailing together for 10 years. In that time they've competed in most of the annual Catalina 22 Nationals. "We've placed in the top 10 several times," Pam says, "but we're still trying to win a first place." That was before results of the 2001 Catalina Nationals were finalized.

"Actually, we each have a Catalina 22," Pam grins.

"Mine is named 'Cattitudes' and I skipper it, with Dennis as crew, in local and regional races."

In national races Dennis skippers his boat, "Tar Baby," with Pam sailing as crew. She is enthusiastic in portraying the satisfaction of sailing and competing together as a couple. It's not unusual though, she admits, to hear the one serving as crew mutter, "Whaaaat? You're going to tack now...?"

Moreover, Pam Slaton is Commodore of the Catalina 22 National Association. At the opening meeting of the 2001 regatta, held in June in Fort Walton Beach, Florida, she was re-elected for a second two year term heading the 1150 member group. "We've got members from most of the 48 mainland states," Pam cites.

Hal and Sally Smith, home ported in Easley, South Carolina, have been a dedicated, highly active, family team in Catalina 22 racing for more than 20 years. Sailing their boat, "Nauti Love," they won the 1981 national championship. This year Hal and Sally made the long drive from South Carolina not to race, but for Hal to serve as Race Manager for the 2001 nationals. They responded at the behest of T.B. "Beattie" Purcell, race committee chairman for Fort Walton Beach headquartered Catalina 22 Fleet 77, host for the regatta.

Hal Smith is highly enthusiastic in describing Fort Walton Beach waters as a Mecca for boating and racing. "The Fort Walton Yacht Club has one of the greatest locations for sailing in the southern United States," Hal asserts. It's a blessing local sailors have long enjoyed, one that is becoming far more widely known. In fact, the Corsair National Regatta was held at the FWYC just a month before the Catalina 22 Nationals.

Shelter and access are the two great enablers. The FWYC fills Smack Point, a snug peninsula facing the western end of 30 mile long Choctawhatchee Bay. The Club's west side is tucked to leeward, with near perfectly sheltered docking facilities for more than a hundred boats. It is the most delightful of waterfront settings, a mile wide stretch of protected water on Garniers Cove providing lavish room for setting sail, mooring, and hurricane anchorage.

A few moments sail around the end of Smack Point put Catalina 22 National sailors in the big waters of the Bay, with the closest point of the race laps an easy 1½ miles or so from club facilities. The course, covering more than 4 miles, designed to challenge both windward and leeward sailing skills, was laid out in a stretch of Choctawhatchee Bay between the cities of Fort Walton Beach and Destin. Ocean winds from the Gulf of Mexico rush free, unfettered, over a low, narrow stretch of barrier sand called Santa Rosa Island, making the west end of the Bay an area gloriously endowed for racing sails.

"During the 2001 Catalina National race week, though," says Hal Smith, "we were chastened with very light to moderate breezes, 3 to 4 knots in the morning, building to 8 or 10 knots in the afternoon." Ten knots of wind is enough to make for a more exciting race, with the nimble, swing keel, Catalina 22's heeled near rail down. Even with light air, sailors were able to squeeze in extra races earlier in the week, changing Thursday to a free day with time to rest up for the annual social hour and awards banquet held that evening in the Fort Walton Yacht Club dining room and lounge.

39 boats competed for the 2001 Catalina National Championship at Fort Walton Beach. 33 in the Gold (championship) Class, 6 in the Silver (Novice) Class, and 10 in the Spinnaker Class. 9 of the Spinnaker Class crews also competed in the Gold Class. "That's a somewhat fewer number than usually compete when the location of the National

Championship falls to a more central part of the Country," Hal Smith says. "Often we look for 50 to 70 boats competing."

The Fort Walton Yacht Club, and it's sailing milieu, are not alone in gaining nationwide attention. In a couple of decades, the once tiny towns of Fort Walton Beach and Destin, the heart of Northwest Florida's beautiful Emerald Coast, have soared in national eminence with mushrooming growth, miles of luxury high rise condominiums, ocean front mansions, fine restaurants, sprightly nightlife, elegant shops, deep sea fishing and diving, and one of the busiest small city jet ports in our Nation.

Fast becoming acclaimed as America's new Riviera, Fort Walton Beach and Destin are often now the confidential destination of Hollywood celebrities and well known business moguls from major cities in the South and Midwest. Despite astounding growth and opulence the area has maintained legacy as a family vacation spot for more than five decades.

And speaking further of families. Marilyn and John Boemer of Roanoke, Texas (in the Fort Worth-Dallas area) won the Catalina 22 National Association's award as "Racing Family of the Year" at the 1997 annual regatta. This year, at Fort Walton Beach, Marilyn skippered their Catalina 22 "Calypso" in the nationals with John, and granddaughters Danielle and Jamie Pickard, as crew. "I've been sailing for 38 years," she says, "but John had never sailed when we first met." Now they've been sailing and racing together for 21 years and owned "Calypso" for 19. As with many Catalina 22 sailors they've not yet won the "big one", but have plucked off several trophies among top five finishers.

"Even without the 'big win' we greatly enjoy racing, and the family-like sense of the organization itself," Marilyn expounds. "We always look forward to renewing old friendships at each year's national regatta." Asked how they decided that she would be "Calypso's" skipper, Marilyn explains that teamwork is what makes families and racing sailors. "We soon found John was really great at sail handling, and with my long years of sailing I'd gained a lot of steering skills. We're just each doing what we seem to do best...and having fun."

That same Catalina 22 devotion and camaraderie seemed evident in every racing crew we interviewed. Gene and Kathy Ferguson of Arlington, Texas have sailed and raced together for 24 years. During that time they've owned two Catalina 22's. "At first we owned a fixed keel boat," Gene says. "But as we got more active in racing we found we needed the swing keel model." Most racers sail the swing keel because it is so much easier to trailer while traveling to regatta locations. "For the past 6 years," Gene adds, "we've raced with our good friends Greg and Lisa Woolsey as crew, in addition to Kathy." Most Catalina sailors race with just two or three on board because of the weight factor in a boat of limited size. Spinnaker racers often sail with three because of the extra need for sail handling. "We enjoy sailing together so much, though," Gene says, "there's no way we could leave either Greg or Lisa back at the dock when we head out for a race." In their case, the fourth crew member is clearly an asset. Gene Ferguson, Kathy, Greg, and Lisa, sailing "Bulletproof" won the 6th place trophy out of 33 boats in the 2001 championship event.

Not only are families and friendship notable in Catalina 22 racing. The wide variety of ages seen in contenders says a great deal about the sailing potential of the boat and the esprit de corps within the association. Joe Becker of Tulsa, Oklahoma has been a member of the Catalina 22 National Association Since 1970, sailing in 23 national regattas during that time. In the 2001 championship at Fort Walton Beach, Becker, sailing his boat "Luff Affair" placed 14th out of the 33 boat Gold Fleet and earned the association's Lifetime Achievement award. Joe Becker is 83.

Sailing is a passion that seems magnified as children of racing families grasp it. Gerald and Jennie Hayslip of Farmers Branch, Texas (near Dallas) have been sailing together for 30 years. They joined the Catalina 22 National Association in 1975 and have sailed their boat "Endeavor" in 19 national regattas, including the 2001 nationals at Fort Walton Beach. Gerald served as Commodore of the National Association in 1988. "We traded up from a 16 foot boat to the Catalina 22 so our three children could bring friends along when we sailed," Gerald says.

Their son David began sailing at age 12 and bought his own Catalina 22 "Enterprise" at age 23. "Now," says Jennie Hayslip proudly, "David has won the Catalina National Championship 4 times and placed 2nd another 4 times."

Race committee chairman, T.B. "Beattie" Purcell is one of the most fervent boosters of Catalina 22 racing in America, and one of the most knowledgeable sources of information on the boat itself. He has been an active member of the Catalina 22 National

Association since 1977 and skippered his boat "Fandango" in many national regattas.

Moreover, Beattie is a retired management executive for Catalina Yachts. His wealth of experience began with Catalina's startup in 1962, following his emigration from Carrickfergus in County Antrim, Ireland. Purcell has sailed from early years and keeps abreast of race statistics for his Irish friends on their Internet web site.

15,000 Catalina 22's have been built, according to Purcell. "There are sound reasons for the boat's immense popularity," he says. "It is reasonable in price, strongly built, durable, and relatively simple to maintain. The boat is very responsive, nimble, stable and forgiving under sail. It is fun to race, and with the four berths it is an effective cruiser. The swing keel model can be trailered with reasonable ease, and pulled up on a beach or anchored in shallow water for swimming, even wading."

The Purcells are another two generation Catalina 22 racing family, having won the award as "Racing Family of the Year" at the 2000 nationals. As race committee chairman, Beattie did not compete in the 2001 Catalina Nationals. However his son Brent skippered his boat "Fandango" in the race, with son Glenn, and Tara Link of Pensacola, as crew.

Preparing for a big national race is exhilarating for those in the local community, too. In a news feature article about the Catalina 22 National Regatta, Mladen Rudman, outdoor writer for the Emerald Coast's Northwest Florida Daily News found racer Bob Lisher of Saint Louis, Missouri standing on the deck of "Yankee" which he sails with his wife Nancy.

"The racing sailor," Lisher lamented, quoting an old adage, "drinks often from the cup of humiliation." He then added quickly, "We don't usually finish too good, but we love sailing." Out of a fleet of 39 racers, that speaks of the fortune of most, at least until another race day.

As with other families, it was Nancy who introduced Bob Lisher to sailing. "It's been a nice family activity," Nancy says. "We have four children and they all sail."

As it turned out, at the end of the seventh heat, when the sea spray had cleared from Choctawhatchee Bay Commodore Pam Slaton and her husband Dennis, sailing his boat "Tar Baby," had earned the first place finish they have worked for so long. They're winners, National Champions, of the 2001 Catalina 22 National Races.

Just ahead of 6th place winners, Gene and Kathy Ferguson sailing "Bulletproof"; was 5th place trophy winner Mickey Richardson sailing "Mischief"; 4th place winner Alan Jepson sailing "Lil Fly"; 3rd place winner Pete Harper sailing "Hummingbird". Runner up, 2nd place winner in the National Catalina 22 Racing for the year 2001 was Keith Bennet sailing "Screamin".

Fort Walton Beach sailor Sandy Zevin handily nailed 1st place in the Silver (novice) Class sailing his superbly renovated boat "Stardust". He won not only the 1st place trophy, but every one of the 7 heats. National Association rules automatically move a novice winner into the championship class in any future races.

Long known for sailing with his wife and daughters as crew, Zevin could be thought of as a novice only in the Catalina 22. He is regarded as a highly aggressive and successful racer in cruiser class and other local races by Fort Walton Yacht Club peers, who opine that he may be a hot contender for the national championship if he elects to enter future nationals.

The 1st place trophy in Spinnaker Class was won by Pete Harper sailing "Hummingbird" Along with his 3rd place win in the championship event, it made for a notable race week for Harper and his crew.

And by the way, the 2003 Hobie Catamaran Junior National Championship Regatta was also sailed in the Emerald Coast's magnificent Choctawhatchee Bay waters, and headquartered at the Fort Walton Yacht Club.

CLIFF HANGING CONDO OWNERS
OUTWIT TRASH RAIDING RACCOONS

"On a clear day," says Pete Gaston, 23 year manager of Stonedge Village Condominium, "our owners can see near a hundred miles." Stonedge Village is perched on the east brow of Lookout Point,1200 ft or so - and nearly straight up - above the city of Chattanooga and the Tennessee River. "We have about a 200 degree, breath-taking, view," Pete continues, "with at least four states in sight." The summit is also historic, remembered as the site of one of the most intensely fought battles of America's Civil War.

Stonedge Village's 11 high mountain acres are the setting for 48 finely appointed, 2,000 to 4,000 sq. ft, domiciles crafted in the serene aura of colonial Williamsburg. Homes are designed in clusters of 2 or 3 and, to the casual view, seem to jut out from the cliffs. "Actually," says Pete, "most have a nice back yard leading up to the edge of the mountain and the first decline is only 30 or 40 feet."

Although a suburb of Chattanooga, the area has been incorporated into the town of Lookout Mountain, Tennessee, and most residents are retired business professionals from the city. Clubhouse, board room and office areas for the condominium are located in a separate building, originally built and operated as a restaurant. "Another interesting thing about Stonedge," Pete explains, "is that our original developer was Robert M. Davenport, widely famous as the founder of the Krystal Hamburger restaurant chain." Davenport was fascinated by the high-mountain acres which was then the site of a massive home owned by J.B. Pound, which he called the Spanish Castle.

Most multi-home developments deal with maintenance dilemmas that are specific to location. Stonedge Village's site puts it often in clouds, so humidity is one special problem faced by community leaders. "Our board," Pete expounds, "tried fiber-cement siding, but found it heavy and hard to handle, therefore

27

too expensive to install." Vinyl might be ideal but owners and board members felt it not in keeping with Stonedge Village's colonial look. "We just went back to using natural rough-sawn wood siding that matches the original," Pete explains, "and we've found that mixing mildecide into the paint is very effective in managing mildew and rot."

At their architect's recommendation, board members have replaced the original Cedar, wood shake, roof shingles with look-alike man made materials that promote longer life and fire protection. "It's probably best," Pete says, "to install them over slats that allow breathing, rather than over sheathing and tar paper that may promote rotting."

In an effort to maintain the colonial appearance, air conditioning condenser units were originally concealed under houses. As units have reached the point of replacement, owners have been encouraged by Stonedge Village's board to locate them outside wherever possible. "We build attractive wood fencing to blend the units in with surroundings," Pete says. "By doing this we've been able to make big gains in air conditioning efficiency and energy cost savings."

Another location-specific maintenance dilemma is the hilly nature of the Lookout Mountain area. Stonedge board members are planning for the re-paving of Village streets. "With all the interest in health and fitness activities," Pete explains, "we've found that loose pea-gravel on these steep streets can be hazardous. Joggers or walkers can find their feet suddenly flying out from under them, so we're planning for a safer paving mix."

Pete expresses pride in a board of directors that is always open to more efficient, cost effective maintenance methods, the most challenging of which can be the restoration of wood building components and trim.

"For instance," Pete says, "Ed Spurgeon devised a method of replacing window sills without taking out the entire window as we'd been doing for years." Spurgeon is Stonedge Village's Maintenance Supervisor and skilled carpenter, as well as a minister in off duty hours. "That saved us a lot of man hours and money."

"If you can be known for one success," Pete laughs, "I'd like to be known for outwitting our trash raiding raccoons." Lookout Mountain, Tennessee and Stonedge Village apparently have plenty of them. "What we did," Pete elaborates, "was to build small, locking access doors to trash containers inside the garages." Gaston crafted a system whereby Stonedge employees collect the trash, separate recyclables, and deliver it to larger, raccoon protected, containers for pickup.

Another effort, one Gaston counts as a major achievement, was in transferring responsibility for the operation and maintenance of Stonedge Village water lines to the local, quasi-governmental water company. "I was able to show them," Pete says, "that our home owners are major taxpayers, just like non-condo home owners, and due the same public benefits." It is a sensible approach, catching hold among many community association leaders. "Otherwise," says Gaston, "condo owners are hit with double taxation...once to pay the taxes, and then, to pay for maintenance of water lines that other citizens don't have to pay for."

Pete Gaston, now 64, doesn't admit to being a body builder, but lifts weights and works out every day. He also has long been an amateur song writer. "I've written hundreds of songs," he says, echoing most writer's lament, "but have never been published." Nearby Nashville, he figures, already has too many professional song writers standing first in line for publication.

Stonedge Village manager since January 1977, Gaston is planning for semi-retirement. He'll continue to work two days a week, personally handling bookkeeping and budgeting, giving Ed Spurgeon, who will be promoted to manager, a year or so of on-the-job guidance.

FACING A KILLER HURRICANE!

In the face of a major hurricane, responsibility for the condominium, it's owners and guests, must come first. Storm preparation at oceanfront Holiday Surf & Racquet Club took 15 hours of October 3rd,1995. After that long day, from 10:00 p.m. until midnight my wife, Sandee, and I worked feverishly in rain and wind gusts to cover tall plate glass windows on our barrier island home. It was the only personal preparation we had time to make. We paid dearly for the lack of it.

At 4:30 the next morning, after four hours sleep, we turned on TV and found to our utter dismay that Hurricane Opal's winds had increased to 150 mph. Unheard of on Northwest Florida's Emerald Coast, it had become an extremely dangerous force. We knew it could mean nothing less than catastrophic damage and life peril. It had aimed straight for us over several previous days and held on a direct course toward our homes and businesses in Fort Walton Beach and Destin.

I rolled into the condominium parking lot at 5:30 a.m. relieved to find that staff members and housekeepers were showing up for work. As General Manager, I was glad I'd adopted a tough attitude toward employees who failed to come to work during hurricane threats.

When weak Erin, a minimal hurricane, hit just two months earlier none of my employees came in. I'd found myself alone to handle hurricane preparations for 166 condos, to try to calm more than 200 people, many of whom had never seen a hurricane. It was an impossible task and left far too many of those 200 frightened, angry, resentful.

By those early morning hours of October 4th, Hurricane Opal was far from a minimal hurricane. It was a rapidly approaching killer!

In the frantic hours before a storm hits there's nothing more reassuring than a hurricane checklist, prepared well ahead of hurricane season while there's time to think clearly.

Ideas should be welcomed from board members, owners, department heads, and every employee. The completed checklist should be studied and discussed at staff meetings. Department managers should memorize assigned duties. Every hurricane season the checklist should be thumb-tacked on a bulletin board and reviewed again with every staff member so each knows exactly what to do.

Every facility is different. The checklist should be keyed to the specific needs of yours. Here are some ideas from our checklist

All corporate records, financial files, office and computer equipment, lobby furniture, movable telephone system components, video rentals, and beach equipment were safely relocated to higher floors.

Elevators were protected by locking them at higher levels. 142 air conditioning-heat units in homes on upper floors were saved by shutting down the central circulating fluid system. Potable water booster pumps, high above the reach of the sea, were saved in the same way. Most of these expensive items would have been damaged because all were connected to ground floor facilities which were destroyed.

We shut off electrical systems, taped glass windows, secured every item which could be blown away, and shut down the pool filtration system. Recently installed doors on upper floor lobbies held, saving carpets, lighting, and elevators.

Throwing deck furniture in the pool won't protect it.

That's ok for the "normal" hurricane of 80 to 100 mph. In the killer hurricane a beachfront pool will fill with sand.

At 6:00 p.m. the day before Hurricane Opal struck, an Emergency Management Agency alert warned of a planned evacuation order. In the frantic stress of the morning, we were glad we'd worked four extra hours to pre-warn guests and owners the night before. Not only had the hurricane gained frightening strength, it was moving even faster giving us far less time. We were glad many owners and guests had chosen to leave the night before.

In the final evacuation, we telephoned every home again. Over and above that, we assigned two person teams to open every door in the seven story building, search the unit, and report the status of each. That gave us double assurance that every home was checked, every person accounted for. Management of life protection should not be delegated. The manager should handle the list of inhabitants, assign phone callers and hall teams, and receive and check off the information that each unit is clear. This is serious business. In Hurricane Camille on the Mississippi coast twenty-six people having a "hurricane party" lost their lives when a condo collapsed.

We reviewed the in-house list for people who might be ill or disabled, or those who might refuse to leave because they did not understand the danger of a major hurricane. We discovered a kidney dialysis patient and her elderly father who had made an unannounced, last minute, decision to stay in their condo during the storm.

As it turned out, Hurricane Opal hit us squarely. Damage was catastrophic, far worse than any of us imagined. Holiday Surf & Racquet Club, along with hundreds homes and condos on Destin's Holiday Isle, was completely isolated for a week. There was no electric power, water, telephone, or sewer service for weeks. Needless to say, the kidney dialysis patient and her father were overwhelmingly thankful that we found them and convinced them to evacuate.

Rather than decrease from 150 to 120 mph as Hurricane Opal luckily did, a killer storm can rapidly increase to as much as 200 mph like Hurricane Camille on the Mississippi Gulf coast in 1969. Despite the tremendous force of wind, it is the storm surge, the enormously rising tide of raging waves, that causes most of the devastation. Opal's storm surge was 13 to 15 feet above normal. Although one Fort Walton Beach weather station reported single gusts up to 144 mph, Hurricane Opal could have been far worse. The storm surge in Hurricane Camille was 26 feet.

When winds abated beachfront and barrier islands were places of unbelievable devastation. Damage to most beachfront condo properties was catastrophic at the first floor level. Front walls, interior walls, furniture, and appliances were driven by pounding waves into a pile against back walls, and in many cases, on through into the parking lot. Lobby doors were shattered. Sand was piled inside two to four feet deep. All electric machinery at ground level was ruined by salt water. Most oceanfront fences, boardwalks, grass, and shrubbery were destroyed. Parking lot paving was severely damaged. Pools were filled with sand, filtration systems destroyed, and most roofs were blown off. Engineers reported that foam type roofs performed especially poorly in hurricane winds. It took months to rebuild homes and businesses and virtually no furnishings or personal possessions at the first floor level were saved.

For the week our homes and businesses were isolated hundreds of FEMA workers patrolled the barrier islands to prevent looting. Engineers evaluated every structure for safety and buildings were searched for dead or injured. Frankly, we were amazed that none were found. Mountains of beach sand were bulldozed from buried streets so utility repair could begin. Police patrols continued for months as residents salvaged what was left and rebuilt. FEMA (the Federal Emergency Management Agency) was criticized for slow and inadequate response after Hurricane Andrew in Miami.

On our Emerald Coast, FEMA's response to Hurricane Opal was immediate, the next day, powerful, competent, organized, thorough. FEMA and local policemen, firemen, and our Emergency Management Agency brought order out of chaos, much needed aid.

Hurricanes, like any catastrophic natural event, are unpredictable. They may lose strength or veer off to another landfall, but there's far too much at stake to ignore vigilance and preparation.

Moreover, a manager must evaluate the storm track and be prepared to make a lone evacuation decision. Many association directors live out of town, not available to guide the decision. In Hurricane Opal our board president, who lived in town, never came or even called to ask what we were doing to protect $14 million worth of association property and the lives of hundreds of guests and owners. Resident directors were among the first to evacuate. EMA officials are often hesitant to order an evacuation. Political criticism because of business losses can be sharp if the storm does not strike. We found them waiting until the last minute and then ordering a "voluntary" evacuation, dangerously dumping the real decision on dozens of large facility managers with responsibility for thousands of people.

Of course each manager faces the same sweaty palm, cliff hanger, "damned if you do, damned if you don't" decision, sharply increasing the risk of someone making a terrible mistake. Even worse, when the critical decision point arrived we found the Emergency Management Agency's phone constantly busy, making EMA advice unavailable.

Even worse, in the rare instances when we could get through, a meaningless recording gave outdated information.

It will help to have a network of six or eight neighboring managers working together to assess the storm threat. We established a larger group of beachfront condo and hotels through our Tourism Development Council to demand firm decision making and effective communication from the local EMA. We shared the cost of several multiple-send fax machines and arranged to staff them in the EMA office during storm threats.

A dismaying factor of hurricane watch is that every news source gives a different location, landfall, and wind strength prediction for the coming storm. Stay with a battery powered radio and select a station that has demonstrated reliability. Use it for all storm tracking information. Once-a-day newspaper reports are not enough and when the power goes off, as it surely will, the TV goes with it. Watch all hurricanes coming across the Atlantic Ocean and track coordinates several times a day for any storm that approaches the Atlantic or Gulf Coasts. Islands of the Caribbean are especially vulnerable.

Longtime Floridians always have basic hurricane rules. If you live on waterfront, get out! A 100 mph hurricane may be survivable, but no one can predict it's increase to150 mph or more pushing a 15 to 25 foot wall of raging ocean. Mobile homes are not safe. Hurricanes breed tornados, so be alert and take shelter in the strongest part of the building you're in, away from windows. Don't be fooled by the quiet and sunshine in the hurricane's eye...the violence will be back. After the storm, stay away from power lines, weakened tree limbs, signs, carports, and other objects that may fall. Be alert for snakes in wet, low-lying areas and watch for nails and glass on the roads.

After the storm, there are things a manager can do while waiting to get back to the property. The day after the storm I arranged to hire a structural engineer, pending approval of the Board of Directors, before he became inundated with work. I knew we'd need a professional to assess safety of the seven story building. I had office telephone lines connected to voice mailboxes at the phone company's office with a message outlining what we knew of the building's condition for out-of-town owners. A second line carried reservation status messages for vacationers. Both were updated as new information became available and I arranged for long distance phone cards so I, and staff members, could respond to owners and guests. We filed insurance claims and reviewed procedures for this unusual situation with our insurance agent.

An emergency meeting of the board of directors was held. We met with Emergency Management officials to assess property damage, with staff members to keep them informed, and with the bookkeeper to arrange continuation of payroll from a home office.

Even though Hurricane Opal's winds gusted to 144 mph and beachfront damage was catastrophic, authorities in northwest Florida are beginning to rethink their order for total evacuation of the area. Roads become grid-locked and some people are trapped in cars during the height of the storm. Many evacuees took eight hours to travel fifty miles in bumper to bumper traffic. Away from the flood and waves of the storm surge onto beaches and barrier islands, most mainland buildings were unscathed. In future storms authorities in northwest Florida may order only waterfront evacuations. Your area may be different, so be aware and involved in the assessment for evacuation need. Managers of waterfront condos and hotels should push hard for firm evacuation orders (not voluntary ones) and for effective communication from your local Emergency Management Agency Despite the devastation of beachfront areas there was more good news. In most high-rise condominiums, homes above the first floor came through the storm with relatively little damage despite pounding waves engulfing the buildings. In several associations, bewildered directors failed to repair the roof quickly enough and rainwater caused severe, costly, unnecessary damage long after the storm.

Our experience with Hurricane Opal in Northwest Florida buoys faith that nature's power can be dealt with and damage lessened, or more quickly repaired, through sensible preparation and effective management.

How Condo Owners Can Help
Save Endangered Sea Turtles!

Community associations inundating the beaches of Northwest Florida are, in many ways, engaging and welcome lifestyle evolutions. Some may be condos, cooperatives, time shares, or associations of individual homes. In either case, the size and density of such projects measurably alter the environmental balance of close by neighborhoods, and often the wider world.

There might be fewer than 50 units. More likely there'll be from 100 to 400 homes cleverly designed into limited but delightful space. A need for fresh water multiplies, there is growing sewage demand, sizeable usage of electricity, large amounts of water needed for irrigation, tons of trash and garbage to haul away, heavy vehicular traffic that will affect existing streets, rainwater runoff from huge paved areas that affect the design and capacity of storm sewers.

One thing is certain! Such mechanical and structural obstacles are being anticipated, properly planned, and successfully managed. Community associations are growing rapidly as a vital, exciting new way for humans to live.

But condos often share another impact, one that involves life itself for beings who share this planet with us. That impact most often is found when building is rapidly moving into previously undeveloped land areas, creating a struggle between the need for human abode and the wild life natural habitat.

Nowhere is this clash with nature more direct, or less understood, than in the silent confrontation between huge, plodding sea turtles and massive beachfront development defined by high-rise condos.

"The sea turtle's nesting habitat in the United States," says Lorna Patrick of the U.S. Fish and Wildlife Service in Northwest Florida, " ranges thousands of miles from the Carolinas down the Atlantic coast to the Florida Keys, and across the Gulf Coasts of Florida, Alabama, Mississippi, Louisiana and Texas."

Patrick, a certified fish and wildlife biologist, is stationed in the Service's Panama City field office.

"The turtles also," she continues, "nest on beaches in Hawaii, but, to a lesser extent on the Pacific Coasts of California, Oregon, and Washington State."

"Sea turtles," Patrick acknowledges, "are a severely endangered species." Centuries ago, they roamed our oceans by the millions. Today numbers are greatly reduced, and all of the eight sea turtle species are faced with extinction.

In just one state, Florida, four of those species deposit 40,000 to 70,000 nests per year with about 100 eggs in each nest. Less than one of the 100 nest eggs, often far less on average, make it to adulthood.

Average hatchling size is two inches. Their first one to three years is spent in the shelter of Sargassum Sea grass mats that travel the Gulf Stream. The growing turtles forage for food, such as crabs, mollusks, and jellyfish, in a struggle to survive their many natural predators. They take 20 to 30 years to reach maturity, while total life span is more than 50 years.

Adults measure three feet or more in length and weigh 200 to 350 pounds. "Once they achieve adulthood," Lorna Patrick laments, "threats to their continuance come only from humans."

After hatching, sea turtles spend their entire lives in the sea except for one event that can make or break their very existence. That event is reproduction, the laying and hatching of eggs. The female sea turtle returns once a year to the beach where she was born to dig a nest and lay her eggs. Following a two month gestation in the untended nest, hatchlings tear themselves free from papery egg shells and thrash their way to the sand surface. After nightfall the group of hatchlings burst together from the sand and scramble at once toward the ocean. "Moving quickly from nest to sea," Patrick explains, "is critical to avoid land-based predators and other threats to life."

The growing press of human habitation along our beaches is, in itself, a deterrent to nesting. Most sea turtle nesting and hatching occurs at night, relying on natural seaside light sources such as moon and stars. In fact, disruption of natural light caused by human artificial illumination poses the greatest threat to this endangered species.

"First of all," Patrick continues, "studies clearly show that brightly lighted beaches are avoided by nesting sea turtles. Even if they do come onto the beach they may lose their way back to sea, attracted instead toward human lighting."

Far worse, hatchlings emerging from nests are strongly attracted toward human light, away from the sea's greater safety. Misled, they die from attacks by predators, exhaustion, drying in the morning sun, and strikes by autos on parking lots and roads. Quite literally, a single light left on near a sea turtle nesting beach can kill hundreds of the tiny turtles. Hatchlings attracted to death in the flames of beach bonfires are sad testimony to their strong attraction toward light.

"Virtually any condominium or community association light," says Patrick, "whether it's porch, pool, street, balcony, stairway, walkway, parking lot, security, floodlights, spotlights, area lighting, commercial signs, flashlights, kerosene lanterns, open fires, automobile headlights...even interior lights visible through windows...are known to increase the danger to the lives of sea turtles."

Any large, lighted, ocean front facility is, of course, hazardous. However, because of soaring valuations, most shoreline property is now dedicated to high density development, especially high-rise condo construction, which lowers the per-unit price of high cost real estate.

In "light" of this modern lifestyle progression, what can beachfront community association owners, board members, and managers, do to help endangered sea turtles?

"The most direct and complete way to save the giant turtles," Lorna Patrick suggests, "is to eliminate all human light sources visible from the beach."

From that human viewpoint, however, eliminating all beachfront lighting is far from practical. Mortal safety concerns and the dimension of some lighting effects mean that compromise is essential. Most important to understand is that reducing, or modifying, beach lighting needn't cause extreme inconvenience, or affect human safety.

"Here follow seven ways " Patrick says, "that condo communities can safely help save turtles."

1. Keep beachfront lighting turned off during the nesting and hatching season. In Florida, as an example, the turtle nesting season extends from May 1st through October 31st. Check with the U.S. Fish and Wildlife Service to determine the nesting and hatching season for your beach area. Lights should remain off all night during this period. "Even ones that stay on until 11 pm will still affect about a third of hatchlings," Patrick tells us.

2. Keep beach lights near nesting areas to the absolute minimum necessary. Unnecessary decorative lights should be turned off.

3. Lower, shield, recess, and redirect lights so they don't shine onto the beach. Any light visible from the beach, even light reflected from buildings or vegetation, is likely to affect sea turtles. Lights should be low-mounted and pointed downward.

4. Security lights should be regulated by motion sensitive switches that keep lights off unless someone approaches the guarded area.

5. Apply dark window tinting to windows visible from the beach, and close curtains after dark.

6. Replace lights with ones less detrimental to sea turtles. "For instance," Patrick says, "studies show that low pressure sodium vapor lights affect turtles much less than other light sources because they emit a pure yellow light that does not appear bright to sea turtles." Yellow incandescent bulbs called "bug lights" work well, too, if kept at low wattage. Lights harmful to turtles include white incandescent, high pressure sodium vapor, metal halide, fluorescent, and mercury vapor.

7. Volunteer your time to help endangered species. A fine precedent is the South Walton Turtle Watch organization of Walton County on Northwest Florida's Emerald Coast. "What we do," says President Sharon Maxwell, "is locate sea turtle nests. We mark them, protect them until hatching, and if necessary help the hatchlings make it safely to the water."Three days after hatching the volunteers excavate to record data on how many eggs have hatched and to release any hatchlings still trapped in the nest.

"Another important thing," Maxwell adds, "is to remove beach chairs, umbrellas, toys, and equipment from the beach at night, cover any holes or tire tracks in the beach, and remove any man made trash."Sea turtles often mistake plastic debris for jellyfish. Eating it will kill them.

"U.S. Fish and Wildlife Service specialists, along with citizen volunteers like Northwest Florida's South Walton Turtle Watch, are working to save endangered sea turtles," Lorna Patrick concludes. "But, we can't do the job alone. We need the understanding and help of everyone who lives, works, or vacations on America's beaches."

FAIR LIMITATION OF DISCUSSION
MOLDS MORE EFFECTIVE MEETINGS

More than a few in the large annual-meeting crowd were noisy, unruly, even hostile. Loud comments and raucous demands to speak caused constant interruption, shredding the meeting agenda.

Adding to the contentious atmosphere, a pair of young men, weight lifter's muscles bulging out of tank top shirts, yelled loudly and shook fists at the president and board members who were attempting to conduct the meeting. As the abusive two sipped beer from an ice bucket on the chair between them, their disruptions became louder, comments more threatening. The president, lamely, even a bit fearful, adjourned the meeting twice to try to regain order.

There were, to be fair, legitimate reasons for owner concern. The 148 unit waterfront development - let's call it the Fountains of Fort Walton Beach Condominium - was racked by revelations of severe structural problems. The defects had been hidden from buyers by smoothly assuring condo documents and "certified" engineering studies.

Upon transfer of the association to owner control, assessments had exploded upward from $55 monthly to $130. These were low priced homes, most - except for waterfront units - tagged at less than $40,000. The new board discovered that the developer of the 8 year old apartment conversion had cleverly avoided setting up maintenance reserves required by state law. Roofs, with an engineer "certified" life of 14 more years, were leaking like a sieve, pouring rainwater into electrical junction boxes, posing the threat of fire in the 8 unit wood frame buildings. Support beams bearing the weight of several second story units were found to be rotten, termite infested. No one could be sure how many more were in that condition.

At such a crucial time, association officers and board members urgently need cooperation and support within the context

41

of an orderly meeting. Only in that atmosphere can cool heads and intelligent thinkers seek solutions that are always found, even to fearful problems.

Sadly, though, far too many community associations suffer the assault of aggressive, opinionated hotheads who foment disorder in even routine meetings through repeated interruptions, hogging the floor, and strident in-your-face confrontation.

Most of us, more balanced, calm, reasonable, considerate of others, find it highly uncomfortable to deal with aggressive, abusive conduct without established "rules of engagement" which help to depersonalize hostility.

Florida's Legislature, a pacesetter in the creation and refinement of community association law, provides the legal precedent for associations to set, at least, some limits on disruptive meeting behavior.

Chapter 718, The Florida Condominium Act, more specifically 61B-23.002 of the subsidiary Administrative Code, empowers a community association to "adopt reasonable rules governing the frequency, duration, and manner of unit owner statements at unit owner meetings, board meetings and committee meetings."

In others words in a large meeting, unit owners who wish to speak might reasonably be limited to one or two statements each. However, as to the length of a statement, the rule "may properly limit a unit owner's maximum time" to no less than 3 minutes, as stated in the rule.

In addressing the "manner" of owner statements, it is clear the Florida Legislature also empowers community associations to limit abusive meeting behavior such as yelling, cursing, hogging the floor, and physical threats. Unfortunately, it is just as clear that many association officers don't know this, or fear the potential political consequences of sharply confronting such destructive behavior.

Frankly, though, the only way to deal with extreme aggression, especially physical threats such as those posed by the two drunken weight lifters, is to hire a uniformed officer to eject abusers from the meeting. Many diligent board members say that any association, knowingly faced with highly aggressive participants, is remiss in it's duty if it does not furnish the protection of a such a sergeant-at-arms. Without doubt, it is a painful step to take. Unquestionably, though, the maintenance of highly valuable property and finances, along with the peaceful lifestyle of the vast majority of more reasonable owners, demand meetings which are orderly and effective.

In a recent poll, the national Community Associations Institute found that 26% of owners in community associations are "somewhat, to very, unhappy" with their home/association environment. Can you imagine the misery if that many individual home owners all over America were unhappy with their homes? Knowledgeable industry insiders say that tempering destructive, aggressive behavior of the few would bring the "very happy" community association home owner ratio to near 100%. Florida Law gives community associations the power to notably improve this widespread problem. The courage to apply discussion limitations lies with association leaders.

While providing associations the means to control abusive meeting behavior, Florida Law strongly protects the right of all owners to participate. "Every unit owner," Florida Law states, "who so desires may speak at any meeting, and no rule shall contain a limitation on the total number of unit owners authorized to speak at a meeting."

However a rule "may properly require that a unit owner desiring to speak at a meeting must file a request with the association a reasonable time in advance of the of meeting." This is of great benefit to association officers, as well as all meeting attendees, in setting an effective meeting agenda, in preparing information for subjects to be discussed at the meeting, and in calculating, at least roughly, the time needed for a meeting.

A vital aspect of discussion limitation which association leaders must know in applying the provisions effectively is found in Florida ADC Rule 61B-23.002 (10). "If an association seeks to impose on the unit owners any rules governing the frequency, duration, and manner of unit owner statements, such rules must be first adopted in written form, whether such rules become a part of the board rules, bylaws, or articles of incorporation."

Note: In any State, including Florida, legislation may be modified at any annual session of the State Legislature. Before attempting to apply such legislation to association meetings your attorney should be consulted to determine current status or availability. In States which do not have such legislation, community association groups may want to lobby for it.

Condo Finds Solution To
Destructive Formosan Termites

It was months after Hurricane Opal's big flood," says Sugar Dunes Condominium Association president Ben Holtrey, "before we noticed what looked like rotten wood in the trim of a garage door." Closer inspection of garages, comprising the first floor of Sugar Dunes, revealed something far more perilous was going on.

14 unit Sugar Dunes Condominium is located on the sugar white sands of Navarre Beach, a dozen or so miles west of the Fort Walton Beach/Destin area on Northwest Florida's Emerald Coast. Hurricane Opal hit the area in October of 1995 with devastating winds up to144 mph and an ocean surge estimated at 13 to15 feet high. The wind driven flood drowned barrier islands Navarre Beach, Okaloosa Island, and Holiday Isle beneath 3 to 5 feet of raging Gulf of Mexico waters.

"After a bit more poking around, " Holtrey elaborates, "we discovered we had termites." Even worse, board members of Sugar Dunes Condo found they had Formosans, native to China, and considered one of the most destructive, aggressive species of termites in the world.

"We learned," Holtrey says, "that our frame structure, soaked by Hurricane waters, made a perfect place for them to settle in because these termites need a source of water to thrive."

Sugar Dunes was just the first to spot the far more destructive Formosan termites. Nearby Holiday Inn suffered an estimated $150,000 in damage to an outside wall. A homeowner in the Village at Navarre subdivision spent $40,000 to repair Formosan damage. "Actually, our pest control company didn't quite know what to do at first," Holtrey explains. "They did a regular termite spray, but it didn't stop them."

The voracious Formosan termite migrated from China into Japan, Guam, Sri Lanka, South Africa, and Hawaii. In 1965, it appeared in the U.S. at a Houston, Texas port, brought to the

U.S. by ships carrying infested soil, lumber, crates, or other wood products.

In the next two years colonies were spotted in New Orleans and Lake Charles, LA, Houston and Galveston, TX and Charleston, SC. Well established Florida colonies were found in 1980, 1982, and 1984.

The Formosan is a weak flier, spreading slowly by itself. Migration is hastened by the transportation of materials, and is commonly linked with railroad ties used for landscaping. In the U.S., the Formosan generally has been confined to warmer temperatures of the southeast, though widespread use of central heating, providing warmth conducive to winter survival, may encourage the spread of Formosans to colder areas of the continent.

Formosan termites quickly cause catastrophic damage. "A 2x4 we took out of one garage looked fine on the outside," Holtrey says, "but looking at it from the end, we found it completely hollowed out, just a shell." In fact, while most termites feed along the grain eating the softest portions of wood, Formosans often completely hollow out tree trunks or wood beams, filling the hollow with digested material to form a nest. In Hawaii, where unprotected homes were built over large colonies, records show that Formosans caused major structural damage in 6 months, almost complete destruction of the home in 2 years.

In addition to homes, they've attacked more than 47 species of living plants including citrus, wild cherry, cherry laurel, sweet gum, cedar, willow, wax myrtle, Chinese elm, and white oak. They chew into the bases of poles, old tree stumps, or other wood in contact with soil. In their most aggressive stance, they will construct pathways and nests to the upper stories of buildings. Surprisingly, Formosans are also known to attack (but not eat) thin sheets of soft metal (lead or copper), asphalt, plaster, mortar, creosote, rubber, and plastic in search of food and moisture. Their highly publicized ability to chew through concrete is a fallacy, but Formosans are uncanny in finding small cracks in concrete that they use as foraging routes.

"Since I had more time, it fell my lot to be president and handle the Hurricane rebuilding." Holtrey explains. Navarre took a near direct hit, even more devastating than the two other major Emerald Coast beach areas suffering catastrophic damage from Hurricane Opal. "The board handled insurance reimbursements frugally, subcontracting most of the work ourselves," Holtrey muses, "so when the Formosan termites hit us with another - totally unexpected - bill for $40,000, we were really glad we'd been so careful." By the time Sugar Dunes owners spotted the first signs, far more hidden damage had been done, requiring the replacement of much of the Condo's, ground level, western walls.

It's vital for association leaders to know that building insurance seldom covers termite damage. And even if the board has a pest control service policy insuring against termite loss, it seldom covers Formosans without a special coverage clause and far higher premium costs.

"You've got to watch for these Formosan termites in any wood around you," Holtrey adds. He includes piers, pilings, posts, logs, utility poles, timber in contact with soil, and foam insulation.

"You've got to carefully check wall surfaces that extend below ground," he warns, "because they commonly invade that way, and also through expansion joints, cracks, utility conduits in slabs, and holes for tub drains." It's important to remember, though, that Formosans do not always require a ground connection. Survey data shows that more than 25 percent of infestations found in southeastern Florida are by aerial colonies.

Watch for large flights of Formosans in late spring to summer, small flights in the fall. Inspect outside light fixtures. Formosans swarm at night and are attracted to lights in large numbers. Inspect cobwebs, window sills, and other areas for wings. Using a flashlight and a probe (such as a screwdriver or pen knife), inspect the inside and outside of structures for tunneling and mud tubes. Look for tunnels that disappear into cracks on masonry, in and around doors and window frames, and along siding, or tap and listen for a hollow sound in walls, baseboards, and floors. Check for mud tubes and other evidence in crawl spaces. Termite tunnels may not always be obvious, so it's best to probe for evidence.

"As you can imagine, we were really upset because the termite treatment wasn't stopping them," Holtrey says, "and then we found a new product that does work on Formosans." The method, known as Sentricon* Termite Colony Elimination System, uses a three-step process.

First, it monitors for evidence of termites in the soil around a structure. Second, when they are discovered, the system uses the biology and natural behavior of termites along with a special bait to eliminate the them. Third, bait is then removed and the system continues to monitor for new colonies that may invade the area.

"This technology is completely different from other methods of termite control because it eliminates a termite colony using a minute amount of chemical compared with conventional treatment methods," says George Baker, product communications manager for developer and manufacturer Dow AgroSciences LLC.

"Because Sentricon does not require drilling holes in interior floors or foundations, it's much less intrusive than traditional methods of termite control. In addition, the active ingredient in the bait is used only when termites are present, so it's a very targeted method of control."

"To start," says Holtrey, "your pest control company sets up Sentricon stations in the ground around the outside of the building." The stations, green plastic containers about the size of an in-ground water sprinkler pot, lay flush with the ground. Wood is placed in the container and checked periodically by the pest control company for termites. When they're found, Recruit* II termite bait is placed in only those stations with termite activity. The termites eat the bait and lead nest-mates to feed on it, eventually eliminating the colony. The bait is in the container only when termites are present and colony elimination can be achieved with as little as one gram of active ingredient. Once a colony has been eliminated, a new piece of wood is placed in the station, and the pest control professional regularly monitors all stations for new colonies.

Recruit II termite bait, approved under the U. S. Environmental Protection Agency's new Reduced Risk Pesticide Initiative, contains the insect growth regulator, hexaflumuron, which eliminates termite colonies by stopping the molting process required by termites to grow.

"We believe -at least, we sure hope - we've beaten the Formosan termites," Holtrey says."They're a big threat to homes, and every condo owner, board member and manager needs to know about them. It really does help to know there's a solution to the problem."

Ben Holtrey, retired as a Church of Christ minister, moved to Navarre Beach ten years ago. With his wife Delatha, he's been an owner and board member at Sugar Dunes for 7 years, president of the association since late 1995. In retirement years he remains busy as a working partner in a landscape company.

"One thing I especially like about helping to manage Sugar Dunes and working with many people in the landscape business," Ben Holtrey says, "is that I often have the chance to minister to someone, to speak the word of faith and support that can change a life or help with a problem. It's nice to find that, even in retirement, a minister can continue God's work."

THESE RETIREE'S ENJOY A
SPIRITED CONDO LIFESTYLE!

The 1238 units of Huntington Landmark Condominium in Huntington Beach, California were planned as an exclusive residential community for senior citizens.

"But, our philosophy," says Dale Caulfield, currently serving a repeat term as president of the association, "has always been that a retiree can do a lot more than stare out a window and watch the grass grow." That conviction, under Dale's direction as 16 year chairman of the recreation committee, has spawned one of the most vital, extensive, and varied recreational programs among America's community associations.

Of course, Huntington Landmark boasts the usual amenities found in most community associations: two heated swimming pools, two jacuzzis, a fully equipped gym, tennis courts, and a banquet room for private parties. These basic facilities would be vital in any community the size of Hunting Landmark, which covers four square city blocks of mid-priced (for California) $160,000 to $200,000 homes.

"But, we thought it was important to do more," says Dale. "We set out in the beginning to develop a wide-ranging program of activities that would offer seniors the chance to stay busy, healthy, interested, involved with others, and mentally challenged."

Because of that early people-oriented planning, Huntington Landmark also has a well stocked library, a sewing room, an art room, a wood working shop, and golf putting greens. "Those are just facilities, the hardware," Dale expounds, "what really counts is getting people to use them."

Dale and his recreation committee, with board approval, arranged for the local community college to offer classes at the condominium. Class offerings have grown over the years, geared to the express interests of residents. At present, they include ceramics, painting, poetry, language, and swimming, as well as a variety of exercise classes fashioned for varying levels of physical ability. Most classes are free. "We call Huntington Landmark the prep school for senior citizens," Dale laughs.

To add to the mix, the1700 residents can enjoy horse shoes, badminton courts, and swim exercise classes conducted in the pools. Residents who enjoy the wood working shop make 500 to 600 wooden toys and have them ready for handicapped children by Christmas of each year. Bingo offered on Wednesday and Sunday is well attended, and the bridge group is an active part of Huntington Landmark life. Tennis and golf associations hold regular tournaments, with Dale Caulfield an active participant in the golf group. A video movie is shown in the banquet room one night a week, seen usually by 60 to 80 residents.

"We think," Dale says, "our discussion group, The World Today, might be the most important of all. It gives residents a forum to review and understand local, national, and international events, as well as the chance to express an opinion. It keeps us sharp, up to date, in our thinking."

"Even though we strictly limit owners and residents to the senior age group," Dale explains, "we have an unusually lenient policy that helps keep families together. Younger family members can come and visit for up to 60 days, so it's easy for the grand-kids to visit for most of the summer, or over Christmas and Easter Holidays.

Because of it's orientation toward seniors, Huntington Landmark's buildings were not designed as hi-rise. In fact only two are multi-level, limited to two stories. "All the rest, the vast majority," says Dale Caulfield, "are engineered as 2 and 3 bedroom single story townhomes arranged in groups of 2 to 5 units."

Huntington Beach is located on the Pacific Ocean in Orange County about 40 miles south of Los Angeles. It's known as surf city, the granddaddy of surfing on the U.S. mainland, and is listed as one of America's safer cities, according to Dale.

"However," he interjects, "our board of directors wanted even the ladies of our community to feel comfortable taking health walks any hour of the day or evening." Consequently, the condominium is fully gated, with strong security staffing. "My wife and I enjoyed living in Los Angeles during our working years," Dale says, "but we've come to really appreciate the quieter pace of Huntington Beach and Huntington landmark."

Dale worked for 34 years with the giant retailer, Sears Roebuck & Co, retiring as the Pacific Territorial Controller for all of Sear's soft lines.

During 16 years as board member and chairman of the recreation committee Dale has also served 7 years as board president covering several separate terms. He works closely with the Huntington Beach City Council on senior issues and was instrumental in the successful passage of legislation protecting the status of senior communities.

"We thought we'd lost it," Dale remarks, "when the Fair Housing Act was passed ending unfair discrimination. But, we believe senior communities are not discriminatory. They're a special, needed part of American life, so we lobbied hard in Sacramento." The result of the efforts of Dale Caulfield and fellow lobbyists was passage of California Civil Code, Sections 51.1 and 51.2 which restored the right to maintain residential communities exclusively for senior citizens. The legislation, of course, properly continues the ban on racial, gender, and other forms of discrimination, including age discrimination in the workplace. Many, if not most, other states have followed California's lead, or are considering such legislation.

Caulfield is effusive in giving credit to those who work with him. "Committee volunteers," he says, "are the backbone of Huntington Landmark."

"Dale Caulfield," says Sandy Meyer, General Manager for Huntington Landmark, "is the person largely responsible for the great recreation program we have. And he's always willing to assist in the association office on evenings and weekends if an emergency arises."

Recently, Meyer adds, Caulfield directed traffic and assisted stranded residents when the rain-swollen Santa Ana River caused heavy flooding to the property. "He's always available by phone to listen to resident concerns," Meyer continues, "and he's responsible for creating an alliance with Newport Beach Plaza (a nearby assisted living facility) to provide catering, luncheon, and transportation services to Huntington Landmark residents."

Caulfield has also been instrumental in Huntington Landmark's participation in the city's Civil Emergency Response Team (CERT) which was created to respond in the event of local earthquake emergencies.

Caulfield and Hunting Landmark's board of directors have recently begun a major program of roof replacement for all association buildings. "Our board has been wise in carefully maintaining proper reserves for this purpose," Meyer says, "and the $11,000,000 needed is already set aside." Cedar shake shingles are being removed and replaced with long wearing composition materials that have the same look. The project was planned in 13 phases, with four already completed to date.

Asked about his view of the relationship between the board of directors and management, Dale Caulfield's answer was not surprising to this writer who spent like working years in the same retail management profession. It reinforces the advantage to any community association of having highly experienced, successful businessmen and women as a part of the governing board.

"Our volunteer committees," Dale Caulfield says, "bring invaluable feedback to the board about our resident's needs and desires." The board shapes that into policy and planning, but the burden of day-to-day detail is left up to the management company and General Manager, Sandy Meyer.

"For 25 years, since it's beginning," says Caulfield "Huntington Landmark has had only one management company, Professional Community Management Associates. Sandy Meyer has been with us for 9 years, except for a couple of brief assignments elsewhere. She's an excellent manager and together they have a great deal of skill in property management, and a world of accumulated knowledge of Huntington Landmark itself. Frankly, I don't know what we'd do without them."

WISE LEADERSHIP BRINGS SUCCESS
OUT OF DEVELOPER'S CHAOS

"In a way," says Lou Schnepp, 14 year association president of Snow Lake Lodge Resort, "being in the right place at the right time was the thing that saved us."

At the time Lou was an executive in the San Bernandino County, California Tax Assessors Office. "One of my associates knew I owned three timeshare weeks at Snow Lake Lodge," Lou continues, "and he brought it to my attention that the developer was not paying taxes on the property."

Far more unsettling, Lou Schnepp knew the developer was regularly collecting those taxes from owners, so he began a quiet, behind-the-scenes check into the developer's financial management of the 37 unit, 1887 week timeshare operation.

"What we found was not only disturbing," says Lou, "it presented a major threat to our investment in the property."

Snow Lake Lodge was built in 1981, preplanned and dedicated from conception as a timeshare facility. It is perched at an altitude of 6500' in California's San Bernardino Mountains village of Big Bear Lake,100 miles east of Los Angeles, 40 miles east of San Bernardino. With a population of 20,000, the village lies in the heart of a beautiful, active, four season resort area, with several winter-busy ski areas, as well as swimming, sun-bathing, fishing, and boating on 7 mile long Big Bear Lake in summer.

"Spring and Fall bring us weather that is just wonderfully mild and enjoyable," Lou expounds, "and a lot of people from the big cities come just to lay back and revel in it."

"Actually," Lou explains, "our timeshare is not directly on the shore, but it is within easy walking distance of the lake (the largest body of fresh water in Southern California), the village, and one of the ski runs which reaches another 1,000' higher up the mountain." The units themselves, contained in three story buildings, are comfortable and expansive, and although of single

53

bedroom design, can be closed off to provide multiple-family sleeping privacy.

"As we dug into the situation, problems soared," Lou Schnepp says, "and our financial risks seemed more perilous day by day." Not only was Snow Lake Lodge under threat by the Tax Assessor's office for unpaid taxes, the fledgling research committee which Lou had gathered together found the association to be more than $450,000 in debt.

Equally shocking, the timeshare's furniture had been mortgaged, not once, but twice...to two separate, un-suspecting lenders. Both were threatening to make the units completely unusable by repossessing the resort's unit furnishings which were far behind in mortgage payments.

Sharply compounding the association's financial problem was the fact that many of the owner maintenance fees were in arrears and 40% of the timeshare weeks remained unsold, financially unproductive.

As the mounting, previously unknown, data brought the timeshare's severe financial problems into clear focus, it was Lou Schnepp who determined that action must be taken immediately.

Under his direction, the now expanded research committee became a "Save-the- Lodge" movement. They instituted an in-depth review of publicly recorded condo documents known in California as Covenants, Conditions, and Restrictions (CC&Rs). This was hurriedly done in order to better understand the rights which were left to Snow Lake Lodge property owners.

In leading the study Lou relied not only on his own background in real estate assessment, but sought advice from knowledgeable friends, fellow association members, and professional auditors to assess the status of the property.

As a result of evidence gathered by the committee, the developer filed for bankruptcy in the spring of 1987, and stepped out of the way, transferring complete control of Snow Lake to it's owners association.

Lou Schnepp was then elected as board member and president of the Snow Lake Lodge Owners Assn, a position in which he still serves as of this writing. To accomplish this vital task Lou had to travel the nearly 100 mile round trip from his home twice a month to monitor the timeshare resort.

As the new board assumed management control of thorny problems, two far reaching steps were quickly taken. "In August of 1987, we contracted with Tricom Management, Inc. to help guide us through the financial quagmire," Lou says. "Their professional expertise has been invaluable." Lou and fellow board members also successfully prevailed upon the developer to have assessment fees mailed directly to the association giving them secure control over the central source of association income.

An equally significant early effort was the successful reassignment of property tax payments from association management to individual owners. Property taxes themselves are reasonable, about $30 per year per timeshare week.

"We just found it far more cost effective," says Lou, "for the individual owner to send in an annual tax check rather than have association management collect, deposit, follow up on delinquencies, and maintain records for 1887 separate property tax units."

Other major steps in the turnaround led by Lou and fellow board members were the successful renegotiation of Snow Lake Lodge's debts with lenders, and the location of an opportunity to market the unsold timeshare week inventory, bringing vital cash flow to the association from originally planned maintenance fees and rental commissions.

According to Tricon Management's Jim Stillinger, Lou Schnepp has continued to provide vital management direction throughout the 14 years of his Snow Lake Lodge leadership.

In 1999 Lou and fellow board members began an aggressive foreclosure project on defaulted individual timeshare weeks. "Bringing these defaulted units back into ownership of the association," says Lou, "resulted in 59 sales, bringing substantial funds into operating reserves, in addition to re-establishing the lost flow of maintenance fees needed for day to day management expenses."

Unfortunately, at about the same time, a bulk purchaser of timeshare weeks also defaulted on his agreement with the association, then refused to return inventory to the association, failing to pay assessments on the weeks held, continuing to sell timeshare weeks with clouds on their titles, which reflected poorly on the association. "Once again," says Lou Schnepp, "we had no choice but to go to court."

According to Tricom Management's Jim Stillinger, the lawsuit was eminently successful, strongly aided by Lou Schnepp's familiarity with the financial affairs of Snow Lake Lodge gained over 14 years of service to the association, as well as his personal testimony before the Court. The association was awarded deeds and beneficial interests in all weeks held by the bulk purchaser.

Moreover, that action released a developer's construction debt against the association in excess of $275,000 in addition to a $114,000 monetary and legal fees award.

"Lou Schnepp holds a strong belief in the prudent use of replacement reserves," says Tricia Deschamps of Tricom Management, "to ensure the quality of Snow Lake Lodge property while carefully balancing the need to keep a reasonable level of yearly assessments for owners."

As a result, replacement reserve funding has improved annually and funds are prodigiously budgeted each year on carefully planned improvements. Association members fully renovated 10 units, and are in the process of refurbishing the remaining.

"After years of confronting major problems we can be proud to say," Lou Schnepp concludes, "that Snow Lake Lodge Resort has recently received an award as a "Resort of International Distinction" by Resort Condominiums International."

PRUDENT PLANNING BEATS
$3,200,000 DEFICIT

"It's really a jolt," says Al Hawck, "to suddenly find your association $3.2 million in the hole." Hawck is not only association secretary, but highly active as a board member, having attended every meeting of the Nevada Jockey Club Interval Owners Association since June 1996. That was the year members finally determined to vote owner control, and consequently the time board members received the first audit in the association's history.

"Not only were we surprised to find the $3.2 million shortfall," says Al Hawck, "but all of our time-share units were critically in need of refurbishment and there was no money in our replacement reserve accounts." With the transition, new association leaders found they'd inherited a situation in which replacement reserves had never been properly funded.

The Jockey Club, was developed in 1972 as a 348 unit condominium with 78 permanent residential condos and 270 timeshare units providing the management challenge of more than 14,000 annual weeks of alternating residency. It's 2 bedroom 2 bath units approximate a spacious 1400 square feet of living space and amenities include a swimming pool, exercise rooms, sauna, and an extensive video library.

Many of the more than 14,000 timeshare weeks are deeded to members who own multiple units. In fact two of the five Interval Owners Association board members are Canadians who own enough weeks to spend, at least, three winter months in Las Vegas residence every year.

Located in the heart of Las Vegas' fabulous "Strip," the Jockey Club's two 12 story buildings are trimmed in neon to blend in with surrounding, world renowned bright lights, 24 hour a day go-go, and gaming excitement. "The movie-famed Aladdin Hotel Casino is just across the street," Al Hawck says. A host of others are little more than a seven-come-eleven roll of the dice away.

Not surprisingly, perhaps, well known dare-devil Evel Knievel made national headlines again by jumping his motorcycle from the top of one of the Jockey Club's high rise towers to the other. Publicity would hardly have been favorable had Knievel missed, of course.

"Thankfully, the distance between our buildings was just right for his stunt," Hawck added, "and the association was glad to receive a $50,000 payment for the right to make the jump."

Al Hawck was leader of the first owner controlled board of directors to be elected, and has also served as a director on the Jockey Condo Master Association since 1998.

Board members carefully studied problems encompassing the huge deficit. After reviewing a variety of financial approaches they agreed there was only one sensible solution, though a painful one. "We had a few complaints, of course, but I've got to give our owners a lot of credit for their wisdom and cooperation," Hawck comments. "They approved the board's recommendation for an astounding $5,000,000 special assessment." With the huge debt paid Jockey Club Interval Owners had $1,700,000 left in the bank, but as plans for the needed refurbishing proceeded, that turned out to be far from enough.

"One of our first steps," Al Hawck expounds, "was to bring in Tricom Management to add some professional guidance to our own efforts. In the two years of working through these major problems they've been a Godsend.

"Our success has been through a wonderfully cooperative team approach," says Tricia Deschamps of Tricon. "Al Hawck and other board members worked diligently with us to prepare a five year financial plan to get the Jockey Club back on it's financial feet." The comprehensive plan recommended gradual assessment increases to owners in 1998, 1999, and 2000 with no increases for the following three years. The plan, soundly approved by owners, also called for complete remodeling of the 27 year old units in fiscal year 1999, as well as adequate annual funding of reserves for building exterior maintenance.

"With our plan and a new budget in place we were able to show terrific early progress," Hawck relates. "By the end of 1997 we showed an audited excess of nearly $1,548,000 in the bank, and the auditors agreed to remove an 'ongoing concern' comment from our annual financial statements."

Full remodeling of timeshare units, begun on schedule in 1999, included complete repainting of unit interiors, light construction connected with the installation of new kitchen and bath cabinets, new doors, new sinks with stylish Corian counter tops and shower surrounds, all new carpet and drapes, the replacement of most furniture, and the installation of a new, state-of-the-art, in-house laundry.

"Most everyone was really fired up with the idea of having such a complete renewal of The Jockey Club," Al Hawck says, "but there was one big catch. Costs for the refurbishment totaled an additional $4.2 million dollars and we only had $1.7 million left in the Special Assessment Fund. The board had to come up with some really creative solutions."

"The result," says Tricia Deschamps of Tricon Management, "shows clearly how important good leadership and good cooperation between board members, owners, and management can be in dealing with a tough community association problem." As things turned out, Al Hawck was instrumental in negotiating a $420,000 settlement with the developer, in establishing an ambitious and productive rental program, and in developing a plan to sell delinquent timeshare units.

Even these highly successful efforts were not adequate to fully fund the renovations, so the Jockey Club's board of directors determined to seek construction loans to finish out the project. Through an application and review process with more than 20 financial institutions, Al Hawck was successful in negotiating a $2 million dollar loan at approximately 9.75% interest over a five year period from a local Las Vegas bank.

By the time 1999 drew near a close Hawck, working with other board members, had finalized a 10 year replacement reserve study.

"One good thing," Hawck says, "is that the complete remodeling project allowed the association to catch up on immediate reserve requirements." The plan for future maintenance needs will gradually build replacement reserves through rentals and sales without increasing assessments over the next three years.

At the present time, the Jockey Club's board of directors is surveying owners to consider a small additional Special Assessment to finish out furniture replacement in the timeshare units.

6 Steps to Selecting
and Retaining Quality
Management Staff

In the early years, community association staffing was as simple as running a classified ad and hiring an entry level counter clerk, bookkeeper, or maintenance type who'd work for minimum wage. Owners eager to serve on the condo board felt sure they knew how to "run" one, and wanted no hireling who might suggest otherwise. Why blow money on "training and experience" when they could do it all themselves?

"Over a lot of stressful years," says John J. (Jack) Herring, "much has happened to change the management approach for many community associations." Herring is a professional Human Resource Consultant, Trainer, and Career Counselor specializing in the community association and hospitality industries.

"The marvelous growth of community association living," he continues, "boosted the awareness of a need for expert management to deal with problems in huge buildings and facilities that owners soon found were far different from single homes."

Other factors were soaring property values with a need to maintain them, discord brought on by naive handling of differing view points, and the growth of vacation rentals that demand expert management. Many insiders say that the greatest wake-up calls were widespread financial losses caused by severe condo building decay, mostly due to a lack of expertise by the inexperienced in timely maintenance of high-rise structures and massive machinery.

The need for professional management is now acknowledged by a great many, if not most, community association homeowners. Even more, it is set in law and regulation by states, such as Florida and California, which have large community association populations. With the need for professionalism conceded, how does management find, select, and retain productive, cost efficient, employees?

"In our consulting practice," says Jack Herring, "we demonstrate six steps in the process of hiring and keeping the right people."

Planning is Step 1. Develop a job analysis, Herring continues, including knowledge (what the applicant must know), skills (what he or she must be able to do, including today's technology), abilities (expertise needed to do the job), and physical demands. The last is vital in community associations with broad land areas, multiple sky-high staircases, miles of walkways, and heavy machinery. The job analysis will be your guide in writing a job description which, in turn, will facilitate a list of candidate specifications for the particular job you have in mind. Determine the pay needed to attract your applicant and balance that with a decision on what you can afford. A good way of estimating compensation is to compare pay scales with management friends in nearby associations.

Sourcing is Step 2. "In finding the right applicants," Herring explains, "it's vital to 'brainstorm', to make a list of places where people with skills you need are found. Community associations are logical sources. Don't forget, though, other industries have similar jobs with people interested in a career step-up. For the same reason, it's important not to forget the best candidate may come from an internal promotion.

Before dashing off a newspaper ad, take a minute to mull over ways to best spread news of the vacancy. An internal job posting on the bulletin board may do the trick. Or, you may need to reach out to schools, government agencies, previous applicant files, trade & professional associations, employment agencies, and "head hunter" executive search firms. Publications of community association and other industries are an excellent source. Classic examples are the resumes and management openings found in the pages of professionals industry magazines.

Modern technology, the Internet, gives us comprehensive leads for a job search. These three web sites are great initial sources. Headhunters.com links job seekers in a variety of industries. Monster .com offers more than a million resumes which can be sorted to eliminate those that don't meet your basic requirements. Jobtrak.com links nearly 800 college and university career centers nationwide. There are costs for employer posting on all three, so check them out carefully. Once you've targeted the most effective sources, you're ready to write your ads.

Step 3, Screening applications. "First," Herring says, "is a judicious review of the applications and resumes to quickly weed out obviously unsuitable ones." Ensuing contact interviews of the remaining candidates will narrow the group to 3 or 4. The contact interview may be in person, by telephone, or a new method called video screening. For a fee, far less costly than flying the applicant in, consultants such as Herring will go to the candidates and video tape interviews for you, using a list of your own specific questions.

Person to person in-depth interviews in your office with 3 or 4 of the best candidates will lead you toward final selection. "We feel," Jack Herring explains, "that behavior-based interviewing gives the employer a significant advantage over other approaches. According to Prof. Herbert G. Henneman of the University of Wisconsin-Madison, "Behavior-based interviewing is a thorough, planned, systematic way to gather and evaluate information,"... by eliciting specific examples of past job behavior to predict future performance.

Testing of skills or knowledge which are key job elements should be conclusive segments of the interview. You'll want to schedule a doctor's physical exam where such expense is essential and cost effective.

"An effective check of references," Herring says, " is vital in today's business world." Technology can make this process easier. The flip side is, availability of that information may make an employer liable if criminal or other unsavory backgrounds are not caught to avoid an employee offense. Some industries, nursing homes for example, are legally required by law to do background screening. It's a move that makes sense for community associations in which management personnel usually have access to homes, and are in direct contact with many homeowners and guests.

Evaluating the finalists, Step 4. "At this point," Herring advises, "refresh your perspective by reviewing your Job Description and Candidate Specifications." Reserve judgement until all interviews are done. Compare applicants knowledge, skills, and abilities. "Job-related past behavior," Herring reminds, "is a powerful predictor of future performance." Consult with business associates in other associations who may have interviewed the same applicants. It's vital to consider personal needs, such as hours, location, travel, expectations, to determine your chance of retaining the applicant. "At this point," Herring says, "it's time to make a "go/no go" decision on each applicant. Cross the candidate off your prospect list, or make a firm offer.

Step 5, Recruiting. This may seem out of place here. "But, it's vital to keep recruiting, or 'wooing,' the candidates at this point," Herring warns. "Never forget, it's easy to lose a most wanted candidate who's misinterpreted something and feels the opportunity may not be right." Another stumbling block is that you may be "wooing" a dual income family. 50% of American families have two workers, and the partner may need to feel secure that leaving his or her job is best.

Prepare a written offer reinforcing the balance between what your association can offer and the candidate's career needs. Extend the offer in person. However, this may be done by phone if the candidate is assured that a written offer will be mailed or faxed immediately. The final statement in the offer should be an assumption of acceptance, with a deadline for getting back to you with his or her decision.

If a candidate wishes to negotiate, be open, of course. However, press for reasons why an issue in contention is important to the candidate. There may be other ways to resolve it rather than just giving in to demand. If you're this far along, it's well worth your time to look for a mutually acceptable compromise to any facet of your offer not fully in agreement.

Remember, not every candidate will accept your final offer. Setting your sights on only one of the final interviewees can make your candidate search doubly expensive by having to start all over again. It makes good economic and managerial sense to develop an alternate candidate, the one who comes closest to your first choice, as a back-up. "It's the best argument," says Herring, "for having a search that's carefully planned, with an evaluation and selective process effectively pursued, step-by-step."

Step 6, Retaining good employees. No discussion of recruiting is complete without mention of keeping good employees. Covering all aspects of it could easily generate a separate article, or even a book. "In brief, though," Jack Herring remarks, "there are four significant, easily identifiable factors in retaining the best of your management staff."

First, perhaps foremost, is recognition. It seems a bright side of human nature to yearn to be recognized, especially by the boss, for faithful work, for extra effort, for achievement, for success. Recognition can be as elementary as a call to the office for a personal "thank you", a praising note on the bulletin board, a mention in the employee newsletter, or an employee of the month award. Successful managers keep all four, and more, in their armory of good management techniques.

Equally important is opportunity for growth. It's as simple as promoting from within, and offering whatever possible for career education and personal betterment.

Work climate is ignored at management's profound peril, at the risk of dissension and efficiency stagnation. Happy employees, ones who stay year in and year out, work in an atmosphere of mutual respect, trust, fairness, cooperation, friendliness, and appreciation.

Compensation, surprisingly, is seldom at the top of "retention" charts. It's importance certainly can't be brushed aside. Good managers, though, say that employees who love their work, who achieve in an atmosphere of recognition, opportunity, an enthusiastic work climate, and fair pay, are very slow to leave for a few bucks a week more. "The bottom line," Jack Herring concludes, "is, the manager who does a good job keeping them will spend less time and money in recruiting and hiring."

A Complaining Owner
Helps Solve the Problem!

"Be a part of the solution...not the problem!" It's an old adage, trite perhaps in many circles, but one that still has powerful meaning in the sometimes confrontational relationships between community association owners and management.

When Palty O'Connor became President of Edgewater West Condominium in Gulf Shores, Alabama he was a bit wary of owner and ex-board member William H. (Bill) Brown's complaints about building maintenance.10 story Edgewater West is a condominium housing just 43 units. It's located right on the Gulf of Mexico in Gulf Shore's West Beach area.

"Bill came on pretty strong, pretty opinionated," Palty relates, "his favorite approach seemed to be 'you gotta get the lead out to get anything done!' But, he's a very sharp, take-charge, kind of guy with a lifetime of business management experience, so I figured having his help would be a lot better than fielding complaints."

Bill and his wife Isabel live in London, Ontario, Canada and have owned their unit at Edgewater West for 14 years. Now that Bill is retired they spend nearly three winter months in Gulf Shores, leaving their condo on a rental program from April 1st through Labor Day.

"Palty is right," Bill says, "I had some serious complaints about the maintenance of our building and grounds, and I was pretty vocal about it. Truth is, though, I'd served on the board of directors for a while and I really didn't want to get involved again."

The problem faced by Bill and Isabel, along with Palty O'Conner, and 41 other Edgewater West owners is shared by many community associations. "With just 43 units, we don't have a budget large enough to hire professional, full-time management," Brown laments. "It's vital that individual owners get involved, and routine maintenance is a big concern ." Another problem common to many associations is that 90% of Edgewater West's members are rental owners and live out of town. "Because of that," Bill says, "A lot of owners and even board members have little day-to-day interest in what's going on, except to complain like crazy if something goes wrong concerning their own unit." Palty O'Connor challenged Bill Brown to help solve the problems he was complaining about.

"Well, finally I agreed to get at least a bit involved," Brown continued. "My first idea was to organize a group of owners to do a daily clean-up and inspection of the main lobby, elevator area, walkways, halls, parking lot, and front entrance." As all of us who are involved in community associations know, these are the areas that can make a condominium property look really shabby unless tended regularly. A program was set up that involved several resident owners and a few others who live in nearby cities and visit the condo more often. "Sharing the work load," Brown says, "we set up a rotating schedule so none of us was tied down every day. It worked so well that, before long, we were all really pleased with Edgewater West's appearance."

With success of the clean-up program, Palty O'Connor eventually prevailed on Bill Brown to take the chairmanship of the maintenance committee. Both were in solid agreement. In the salt air environment of a beach front property, routine maintenance is crucial to extend building and equipment life. "I owned and managed an oil distribution business for 40 years," Brown says. "Like most businessmen and women who buy condos, I was surprised at how little cash flow an association has to pay for building and grounds upkeep. We hire a management company to handle our rentals, and we have a full time maintenance man, but someone has to train and supervise, and watch the details." Bill Brown used his years of business experience to set up a maintenance program that gives a sense of direction to maintenance personnel and keeps tabs on the condition of electrical and mechanical equipment, railings that need paint, landscape and parking lot care, and routine touch ups that maintain a high level of community attractiveness. Bill supervises in the winter months and arranged for a fellow owner who lives nearby and visits often to watchdog maintenance activities during other months.

All agree it's working well. "In a big property," Bill Brown says, "one with a full time, professional manager, it's vital to give suggestions to the board and stay out of the managers way. But in a condo the size of Edgewater West, a lot more will get done if owners get involved rather than just sit back and complain."

A Good Manager
Double-Checks!

Even with the best of Board-Manager teams, selecting the right contractor can be tough. It's a management decision that means happy owners and a job well done...or devastating problems and financial disaster.

In a recent assignment Cindy King of Remi Management in Santa Cruz, California proved again how vital it is for a good manager to get up from the desk, go on the construction or renovation site, become familiar with all aspects of the project, and thoroughly inspect all work. Needless to say, it's a wise board whose manager has a construction background or good understanding of construction principles.

A few months after a devastating earthquake, Cindy King joined a management company in Los Angeles. Her task was to supervise several associations, half of which were struggling with major earthquake damage. One of them, an association in the Sun Valley area, was suffering a flood of daily homeowner complaints against the contractor hired by the board to repair damage.

With the advantage of a construction background Cindy handled the problem head-on. She immediately scheduled a "walk-through" with the contractor's supervisor. What she found was not only inconvenience and frustration for owners, but a well-spring of future building and financial problems that were being amassed by contractor uncaring and incompetence.

"As we walked the property," Cindy King said, "I saw dryrot being hidden by new planks and stucco, and termite infestation that was being covered up rather than treated and repaired." She spotted wooden fence slats being attached with nails rather than the proper wood screws. "I asked," Cindy continued, "if the wood being used was water treated." Untreated wood will warp when wet, and nails will pop out. "The supervisor assured me," Cindy stated, "that the wood was water treated, but, after the first couple of rains we had warped boards."

Cindy found that work was being poorly coordinated. Concrete walkways were being poured over damaged electrical conduit and plastic piping. This meant that when repairs were finally made to these items, new concrete would have to be broken up by jack hammers and then poured all over again. Stucco was being reapplied without the power wash that would assure good adhesion. Cracks were being covered up by stucco without epoxy injections needed to strengthen the underlying structural surface.

"So many things were wrong," Cindy continued, "Owners were being inconvenienced by power tools left on sidewalks, and concrete was being poured in front of units without notice. I asked about all of these problems during the walk-through but never got a straight answer from the supervisor. He just diverted the conversation elsewhere. In fact, in daily work there was never a supervisor to be found."

"Even worse," Cindy confided, "I discovered money discrepancies. The contractor had added extra costs, but had not done the work or submitted a change order. I also found the contractor had charged the association twice for the same roof repairs."

Before authorizing any further work Cindy asked the board of directors to join her in an inspection. "We ended up with a list of 102 problems and gave the contractor fifteen days to correct them," she said. "At the end of that time only half of them were done and most of those were wrong."

It seems California's earthquake area was dealing with the same problems Floridians experienced after Hurricanes Andrew and Opal...an influx of poorly qualified, uncaring, and sometimes dishonest workers. But, with management expertise and the advantage of construction experience Cindy was ready with an idea for her board of directors. "I recommended that we bring in another contractor to evaluate the project and the quality of the work being done," she said, "it was one I knew had an excellent reputation for quality work and integrity".

The board was so pleased with the new firm's interview, work recommendations, and evaluation, they fired the previous contractor and filed suit for lost revenues. The new contractor was able to complete the work, right on schedule, in nine weeks...correcting the mess the previous contractor took nine months to create. "It was like a dream not to hear complaints anymore," Cindy said, "homeowners came to board meetings praising the new contractor."

"How nice it is," Cindy says, "to hear a board express such appreciation for a job that finally turned out great. They felt if I had not come along, they would have been left with a building with serious hidden defects and a contractor long gone. Nobody won financially, but it brought the board, homeowners, and the managing agent to a valuable understanding of trust and commitment to each other."

The real moral of this story, though, is that a good manager goes personally to look and inspect every aspect of work projects. In community association management success is a "hands-on" business.

A GREAT IDEA FOR
PROFESSIONAL DEVELOPMENT

Professional development is a career-long process, one which will make or break community association management personnel. It will also enormously affect the community association itself, especially in light of board and owner attitude toward manager retention and expectations of the manager's contribution to substantive decision making.

One state government, Florida, has legislated manager pre-certification study, licensing, regulation, and continuing education. Every manager hired in Florida must meet these standards and every community association with 50 or more units and/or a budget of $100,000 or more annually must hire a licensed manager unless the board chooses to self manage. California has a similar, although somewhat less inclusive, program of regulation.

However, throughout the United States the Community Association Institute's Professional Management Development Program is the backbone of community association manager preparedness. It leads to the Professional Community Association Manager (PCAM) designation.

According to Executive Director, Joseph F. Watt, members of the California Bay Area Chapter (San Francisco) of the CAI have come up with a great idea to encourage manager education. "The Chapter's Board approved it," Joe Watt said, "as the PCAM Mentoring Program and Scholarship Fund." The program was conceived and developed by the chapter's Managers Committee, chaired by Peter S. Williams, and established as an ongoing project. "Here's how it works," Joe explains. "Each chapter PCAM candidate will be assigned a mentor to assist in the successful completion of CAI's educational program culminating in the PCAM award." Even more important, and more unusual, the committee planned a chapter scholarship fund to provide financial assistance grants to managers working toward their PCAM certification and recertification studies. These grants will go to managers who have demonstrated a sincere commitment to success through continuing education.

In a "put your money where your mouth is" effort, the Managers Committee held their first fund raising banquet at the St. Francis Yacht Club, San Francisco, in September 1997. More than seventy chapter members and guests attended. The enthusiasm of Bay Area members toward the idea was clear when the proceeds of the dinner event totaled $7,000 to establish the scholarship fund. "The program was a great initiative of the Managers Committee," remarked dinner speaker Roy Helsing, Bay Area Chapter President. "Associations will benefit immensely from this idea since better educated managers can only lead to even better managed associations."

"Financial awards will be granted to manager candidates on a merit basis," says Joe Watt, "to those who practice management in accordance with the highest prescribed ethical standards." The Bay Area Chapter board of directors has established the fundraiser as an annual event. In a fitting, and rewarding, turn of events, Pete Williams, chairman of the Managers Committee which developed the mentoring program, was awarded the first $450 scholarship.

fort walton beach, florida

VARYING MOTIVATIONS OF
OWNERS AND MANAGEMENT!

It is painful to find oneself wedged between two somewhat challenging, but clearly worthy, points of view. And that's exactly where Managers Report magazine's esteemed publisher, Ivor Thomas, found himself in writing an "Editor Speaks" column. His response was to a heated letter from a group of managers stressing management's side of an issue Ivor wrote about in a previous column.

In that article, as a condo owner himself, Ivor wrote of what looms as powerlessness to many individual community association homeowners. Ivor opined that owners may feel unimportant..., even a nuisance..., to management, with scant respect, and little control over their own home environment. Ivor perceptively explained that management employees should be taught to defer to each and every home owner as a "member of the family who owns the business."

In truth, of course...that's what they are. And a manager or employee who does not respond to the needs and views of every home owner with courtesy and respect will make community association living far less rewarding than it should be.

But, in that same truth lies danger..., far greater to the property and finances of the association. In fact, many community association management insiders view that danger as the last major stumbling block to effective, professional community association management. It has caused the abandonment of community association living and the sale of untold numbers of condo units. It has caused the loss of thousands of excellent community association managers and employees, and millions of dollars in property decay. In far too many associations it has made the education and skill of even licensed managers a farce, and strangled their effectiveness to the detriment of the entire association.

The damage caused to any organization by the dilemma these managers reviewed is far from new in human relationships. Over centuries it has been described in many different ways. "Too many cooks spoil the broth," comes to mind. Or "Too many chiefs and no Indians."

Far more destructive to any business chain-of- responsibility is the derisive attitude many pro-active homeowners and board members hold toward professional management itself.

It's rather nice, many consider, to have a sort of "head clerk" to handle night or weekend problems so "I" don't have to be called out of bed, or when "I" want to take a two month trip.

But, just let any management action "I" disagree with occur...and it's "my" right to personally interfere, even to scream and curse at the manager, or politically manoeuver to have him or her fired, because this is "my home."

Yes, indeed, the community association unit is the home (or second home) of every owner. It is also an inseparable part of a multi-million dollar property with management and maintenance needs far larger, far different, from those most owners will have experienced. Most of all, unit ownership is part and parcel (like a share of stock) of a legal corporation, with great need of a properly functioning chain of responsibility and respect for the rights of all share holders. The protection of highly valuable corporate assets and monies demands management that does not have to be "politically" fearful of doing the job that professional management should do.

But...let's review those concerns as Ivor's letter-to-the-editor writer listed them...

1. Some managers have "more freedom to manage." It's a kind way of saying vast numbers, perhaps most, don't. They're forced to waste time, grin and shuffle, bow and scrape, while "checking" with several politically active owners or board members as to whether they'll be "happy" with what the professional manager knows must be done.

2. Owners "chit chatting," with employees. Employees should never forget that courtesy and friendliness are vital in the owner-management relationship. But every association has an owner or board member - likely several - who bring their coffee to the office of the manager, or "favorite" employee,

and spend a couple of hours every day amusing him/her self telling "old war stories." A board or committee member who needs information should make an appointment, get the info, and get gone. Anything else is "stealing" the valuable time of an employee, time that belongs to the corporation, that is, to all owners. The manager or employee, of course, is afraid to oppose these frustrating gab fests. After all, an insult to "one of the family that owns the company" is far more than likely to result in losing one's job.

3. Owners gigging employees to do personal errands or tasks is the same "stealing" of valuable corporate employee time which belongs to all owners.

4. Boards should consult with the manager as to the legality of their proposed action. Why... for heaven's sake...not? Why pay a management pro 30 or 40 grand a year and not listen to him or her. Do board members, far more likely to be familiar with an individual home, really know more about large buildings, heavy machinery, expansive landscaping, facilities, and staffing problems than a trained, licensed, experienced manager? If they do, they've got the wrong manager. To use Clintonese...it's the team work, stupid!...that protects valuable corporate assets. It's important to remember, though, that in states like Florida it is against the law for even a licensed manager to dispense purely legal advice. That is the purview of the association attorney.

5. Owners should air complaints at board meetings. Employees must...must...respond quickly and surely to every problem or question that concerns any owner. That said...the owner who repeatedly criticizes, nags, yells at, curses, or threatens employees creates the most destructive force in community association living. This is grindingly true when that owner is politically pro-active. Unfortunately, regarding a few, perhaps 1% or 2% of owners, it is all too typical. Yes, such complaints should be immediately referred to the board of directors, who should have a pre-set policy, and written rules, for dealing with behavior which is so damaging to the corporate chain of responsibility.

6. Flack managers get for rules enforcement... falls into the exact same category. Let's be honest, if the board has approved it, the manager and employees should not have to take insults when they're enforcing it...that is, doing the job they're paid to do. Here again, they need the solid backing of the board. If enough owners are unhappy, the board will surely change the rule.

7. The board should create policy and leave day-to-day management to the manager. Of course! Can any corporation...in the real business world...survive when any stockholder can walk into the office and intimidate management? What is often forgotten by owners and even board members... is that a community association is not just a social amusement or retirement hobby. It is a "real world" legal corporation with millions of dollars worth of assets, thousands of dollars in cash flow that must be protected, and myriad, daily maintenance, operational, and employee problems that must be managed. If done right, it is more than a full time, professional job.

Guess who the big losers are when, "too many cooks spoil the association broth?"

Yep, you got it right...it's all the other owners! Good management employees will quickly find better jobs when the day of atonement comes. In a community association, it takes far longer, and thousands of dollars, to reestablish property and social values decayed by failed leadership.

With eighteen years of community association ownership and management familiarity, it seems to this writer that state legislatures must reflect on one more fine tuning of community association law.

To be sure, legal guidelines guarding and defining individual owners rights, and the requirement for management professionalism, are already firmly in place in several states.

What is needed are just-as-firm guidelines... with penalties...that require association owners and board members to adhere to a non-harassed, respected, professional, management format.

In other words... the board sets policy and ensures that policy is carried out. One board member is legally voted as the manager's boss, transmitting policy. The professional manager/ CEO manages the staff and day-to-day operations. No one else "meddles" with the staff.

Can anything be more fair to everyone involved? If it works in the real "corporate" world, do the highly valued assets of "not for profit corporation" community association owners deserve less?

COMMUNICATION
...BUILDS TRUST!

It is quietly well known, but little discussed, in our condo world that a few hostile, belligerent owners or board members can cause severe problems. They likely number only 2% or 3% of unit owners, but their self-centered, fiercely controlling behavior, abuse of others, misguided interference in the management process, creates havoc in many community associations.

Good managers, management personnel, and even association attorneys can be lost. Often the most capable owners won't serve on an association's board of directors because of their disruption and harassment. Some owners just get fed up and sell their units.

But, what of the other 98%, the vast majority eager to work together in an amiable manner to make the association successful? Like all of us, they too, might occasionally seem angry and difficult... demanding attention simply because they have a problem, or need assurance that a project or rule is being handled properly.

Cindy King of Remi Management in Santa Cruz, California has a great tip for dealing with the occasional frustration and stress among people living closely together in community associations. It's not a new idea, but one managers and board members often forget in the fast pace of management responsibility.

"Villa Glen Home Owners Association is a lovely place with 47 units located in Los Angeles near Beverly Hills," Cindy relates. "When I took over as manager I found a group of really upset owners. They felt problems were not being resolved, that there was little personal relationship with management. With my other association responsibilities I was getting 30 to 60 problem calls a day."

"I decided," Cindy continued, "to deal with the crushing backlog of problems and angry owners by handling them head-on, returning every call immediately. I made a point of dropping anything I was doing to answer a call or return a voice mail as soon as I received it. Sometimes, I could solve the problem on the phone or call back a solution with an hour or so."

Homeowners in a community association are no different from customers in any other business. They want to talk to a human voice, not a voice mail-box, and they would like a problem solved immediately...or certainly within a reasonable time frame.

Unfortunately, in the press of association business sometimes same-day problem resolution is not possible. "In that case," Cindy King says, "I always give the owner a time when I will call back...hopefully no later than the next day. Some seem surprised that their call is returned so quickly and usually they're satisfied to wait until I can call back with a solution. Of course, it is vital to keep the promise to call back!"

Managers sometimes forget to take time to be personable with homeowners. "I think of a problem call as a chance to build a personal relationship with my homeowners," Cindy says, "I take time to chat with them and find out how they feel about the property and management. In the annual meeting, I stress the importance of owners and management working together as a team, that we need their help and ideas as surely as they need our management expertise.

"Now," Cindy King concludes, "I get fewer than a dozen problem calls a day. And I've managed as many as 20 associations at a time.

The nicest thing now is that some of the owners are just calling to say...hi!"

POST-TENSION CONSTRUCTION
HIGHLY EXPENSIVE TO REPAIR

"A condo balcony restoration,"says Cheryl Hoste, General Manager of Carlton Place Condominium, "is like the lone logger, trapped by a fallen tree, who had to cut off his own leg to save his life."

Like so many in ritzy Palm Beach, Florida, most Carlton Place owners head north to cooler, seasonal, residences during South Florida's sweltering summer. "We have a world of admiration," Hoste lauds, "for 12 owners who stuck it out with us during "hell summer" with the inconvenience, noise, dust, and plastic covered windows of major concrete restoration."

In fact, Carlton Place's difficulty was compounded by the "post-tension" engineering design used in the original construction of it's twin, 5 story, mid-rise towers. Instead of thick, heavy, static steel rebars, "post- tension" engineering uses much lighter steel cables, stretched taut with tension, to provide reinforcing strength for the concrete building. The system allows thinner concrete slabs, saving building weight and cost.

In a sense it is similar to a cable suspended bridge, except that cables are buried inside the concrete of the building. In the restoration process cables must be loosened, concrete repair done, then bolts tightened again to re-apply proper tension.

In Carlton Place's structure, each major cable carries 90,000 pounds of stress. "When they were tightening the bolts again," laments Hoste, "five of them snapped like a cannon shot and cables hit the wall like a cannonball, knocking out chunks of concrete and shattering windows."

Carlton Place, located directly on the Atlantic Ocean in the southern edge of Palm Beach, comprises 69 notably upscale units, ranging from 2200 to 2700 sq ft. The structures are only 17 years old, first occupied in January 1982. Balconies are comfortable and generous in size, ranging from 300 to 1200 sq.ft.

"The need for major concrete repair," says Hoste, Carlton Place's manager for more than 3 ½ years, "rears its ugly head slowly, rather than in one big surprise." First, she relates, there's a little rust (spalling) here, and a small crack there. Far more noticeable in post-tension construction is rusting of the big, exposed, cable bolts and anchor plates.

"Some buckling of a few balcony tiles certainly seemed more problematical," says Cheryl Hoste, "then our board voted to require that carpet be removed from the last three carpeted balconies. We knew the problem was severe when concrete came right up with the carpet, exposing steel reinforcing cables." Three balconies were redone two years ago, nine others the following summer, leading to the major concrete balcony restoration project this year. "Unfortunately 1999 turned out to be the most threatening hurricane season in many years," Hoste continues, "in fact we had a hurricane warning the day our restoration project began."

After a comprehensive engineering study, Carlton Place's board and manager found that no balcony units would be completely removed. However, balcony restoration was needed on virtually every unit, to remove decayed concrete, sandblast rust from reinforcing cables, repaint the cables with protective primer, re-pour the concrete sections, and reapply waterproofing and sealing materials.

"Generally we found the greatest damage at the outer and inner sides of the balcony," Hoste says, "in other words along the railing and sliding glass doors." However, to highlight the inconsistence of spalling damage, five condos had to have floors cut away 12" to 18" inside the unit to repair decayed concrete and reinforcing.

"On any concrete restoration project, it is vital to have an original set of building plans," Hoste confirms, "to pinpoint exactly where reinforcing steel is located within the concrete slabs." In the case of Carlton Place, board members found that steel reinforcing cables were of different lengths, some stretched across an entire floor slab, while those serving to reinforce balcony areas were much shorter.

The extent of concrete restoration at Carlton Place served as a catalyst for the rewriting of rules and regulations concerning the protection of balcony surfaces. Most owners readily agreed that carpeted balconies will not be allowed. While quite a few floor tiles were removed in the restoration process, owners and the board voted to approve tiled balconies as long as an effective grout seal is maintained to prevent damaging salt water incursion into the concrete floor.

Twenty-one owners were able to retain existing tile balcony floors by replacing tiles damaged in the restoration process. Ten fully re-tiled balcony floors, while the majority of thirty-eight owners chose the more conservative approach, leaving the balcony floor with it's unadorned concrete look and an effective sealant. Based on the new rules agreed upon, any necessary future removal and replacement of balcony floor tile will be at the expense of the individual owner.

Carlton Place's engineer, Cheryl Hoste explains, calculated concrete restoration costs at $432,000, while the board added a cautious 25% overage factor making the initial budget $552,000 plus $20,000 in engineering costs. "The engineer, "Hoste says, "had projected that 67 reinforcing cables were affected by the spalling. It turned out to be 133, with an additional cost of $75,000." Carlton Place's total costs soared nearly 50% over the original budget to a surprising $750,000. "It just points out," Hoste says, "the hidden nature and unpredictability of spalling damage and expense, especially in post-tension construction.

Like many among America's leading industrial families in Palm Beach, Carlton Place owners have preferred to personally invest funds - otherwise accumulated in statutory reserve accounts - more aggressively and profitably than is permitted to community associations by Florida Law. "For that reason," Hoste relates, "owners have historically voted to waive monthly statutory maintenance reserve deposits, instead opting for special assessments when needed. And they take pride in customarily strong support for what the board believes needs to be done."

Cheryl Hoste moved to Florida from Cleveland, Ohio when her husband accepted an engineering position 21 years ago. "Truth is," she says, "like millions of others we just fell in love with the Florida weather." Since then she has managed several properties, including individual assignments, multi-associations, and a large-scale master association, before taking the helm at Carlton Place.

"Early on," Hoste continues, "I began looking for a professional organization with emphasis on education, one that would help me grow as a manger." She first found CAI, the national Community Associations Institute, where she remains active in her local chapter.

She has also been a driving force in the more local, 110 member, Palm Beach Community Managers Association, serving as last year's president. The group meets weekly, instead of monthly, with luncheon meetings that usually comprise a smaller group, facilitating the sharing of experiences, information, and ideas.

"The small group makes it seem realistic to debate larger state-wide and national issues such as beach restoration and the effect of coastal development on Sea Turtles and other marine life," Cheryl Hoste concludes, "But we were really glad to be able to share information and ideas - like preparation and the safety of our residents - when Tropical Storm Irene was bearing down on us this fall. That's when you fully realize how important continuing education and up-to-the-minute information can be."

CONDO DOCTORS
MAKE HOUSE CALLS

It happens hundreds of times a week in vacation destinations all over America. Someone comes back from the ski slopes with a painful, swollen, sprained ankle. Or back from the beach with an agonizing sunburn. Or, perhaps, with a foot cut by a seashell, or stung by the lance of a stingray. Or back from dinner with fiery indigestion caused by unfamiliar, rich food...something the medical professional may call a gastrointestinal illness. With these, and many other similar afflictions, medical attention quickly leaps to the top on a list of planned vacation activities.

It may seem unreasonable, in a sense, but truth is an acute illness or trauma, such as heart attack or a severe injury from a fall, can be handled more readily. The family or the condo's management staff know immediately that 911 must be called. An ambulance will be on the scene within minutes bringing highly trained medical personnel who will take full charge of the medical emergency, including where to go, whom to see, and how to get there.

It's dealing with the in-between conditions that can be the most perplexing on vacation, ailments which can't wait a month for your next regular doctor's appointment back home, and yet are not threatening enough for a call to 911. In other words, urgencies rather than emergencies. Needless to say, the vacationer likely won't know the name of a doctor to call, nor where the nearest medical clinic or hospital is located. And you can bet those facilities will probably be found all the way across town over streets that are totally unfamiliar. It's also virtually a slam-dunk that the condo manager or the management staff will be the nearest thing to a family the vacationer has as a source for quick medical guidance. What happens, almost without fail, is that the ailing vacationer finally finds the emergency room of the nearest hospital and spends hours in it's waiting room. He or she will be medically helped at last to be sure, but suffering the stunning setback of a traumatic, unplanned, wallet-ectomy to his vacation budget.

"We think we have a better idea," says Dr. David Webb of 'Doctors on Call,' a service of Coastal Physician Services of America, Inc. "Would you believe it?" he exclaims, "Our doctors make HOUSE CALLS!" Webb's organization serves Northwest Florida's Destin/Fort Walton Beach area. But the idea has taken hold in a number of other travel destination cities including New York and New Orleans, as well as Florida's Fort Lauderdale, West Palm Beach and Orlando.

"A similar clinic started up in Miami in 1996," says Webb, "and now, three years later, has a staff of 37 doctors."

The idea, of course, is not new. Older Americans remember a time when a great many, if not most, physician appointments were held in the comfort of their own homes where the doctor came to call. The high value of professional time and the need to treat far more patients per hour has changed all that.

And yet, it seems clear that Dr. Webb, along with fellow medical professionals in other widely ranging cities, have hit on a real need for their new/old idea.

Here's the gist of it. Vacationers, of course, cannot all be classed among the wealthy. In fact, travel is far more affordable to a broader spectrum of Americans than ever before. At the same time, most of us who enjoy travel can also afford reasonable medical care when needed, especially when provided in much easier, more effective form. The key words here are reasonable, easier, and effective.

"The cost for a medical house call," says Dr. Webb, "has to be a bit more than a visit to your doctor's office because of the extra time it takes for us to drive to each patient." However, costs for a house call by the condo doctors will usually be far less than an emergency room visit.

"More important, to a great many vacationers," continues Webb, "the ailing patient won't have to traipse all over town to look for medical care, wonder how to find the suitable medical professional, nor wait for hours in an impersonal, crowded emergency room."

In light of obvious benefit to a large, sharply targeted, clientele the slogan for many of the condo doctor groups goes something like this: "Don't spoil your vacation with long waits in the emergency room for medical or urgent care."

"And don't forget," Dr. Webb reminds, "our services are not limited to condominiums. We make house calls to any vacation or travel accommodations including resorts, hotels, motels, and private vacation rental units." In addition services are available to local residents who may prefer or need medical care in the comfort and privacy of their own familiar surroundings. House call medical care may be especially important to winter 'snowbird' visitors who are of the elder, sometimes less mobile, population.

Condo doctors assure a staff of competent medical professionals, prompt response, and house call service from about 8:00 am to midnight, although some larger practices may offer daily 24 hour service. Daytime in-office medical care is also usually available from about 8:00 to 4:00, but it's important to remember that specific time schedules will vary from practice to practice.

Most of the condo doctor groups advertise services for medical conditions including but not limited to: respiratory illness, sore throat, congestion, sunburn, pediatric illness, middle ear and external ear infections, allergic reactions, Asthma, minor trauma, sports injuries, Hypertension, Diabetes, food poisoning, and acute gastrointestinal illness.

In addition many other illnesses laymen think require an emergency room visit may be effectively treated by a doctor who makes house calls.

By far, most, if not all of these new 'house call' physician groups are approved as medicare, workmens compensation, and standard health insurance program service providers. Many are now equally prepared to handle employer services such as drug testing. As a general rule, nationally recognized credit cards can be used as payment for medical services. However, the vacationer should check to be sure as payment formats may vary.

"For the management of a travel destination," concludes Webb, "it's vital to know that properties and resorts which display our medical services brochure assume absolutely no liability for the medical services provided by house call physicians.

Condo Board Members
Find Costly Design Error

In our condo way of life, it's a lesson many of us have learned the hard way. In mid-rise and high-rise concrete and steel buildings, architectural or engineering defects and builder's mistakes, often take years to show up. When they finally become unmistakable, however, resolution is virtually always a major, costly reconstruction.

"I guess we were no different," says Angela Rogers, General Manager of Silver Dunes. "It took us a long time to accept that we had a major problem."

Silver Dunes is 30 years old. Built in 1972, the 97 unit condominium is the oldest in Destin, Florida. It was a noticeable sagging of certain balcony floor slabs and condo unit ceilings, and stress cracks on the underside of slabs, that brought the problem to the attention of owners. That, plus the fact that the infirmity was slowly, steadily growing worse.

The mystifying thing was that only the floor/ceiling concrete slabs separating units on the 4th and 5th floors of two of the six buildings were affected. The other four buildings are two story. "That's probably why it took us longer to tackle the problem head-on," says Angela, "it wasn't general, but confined to those two areas.

President Malinda McCloy and a wise board of directors decided that it was time for a professional engineering assessment of all building structures.

"I'm truly blessed with a great board," Rogers says, "they're very supportive, a sharp group of homeowners who really care about Silver Dunes. They did the right thing in the nick of time."

The board selected the team of Memphis, Tennessee architect Robert Lee Browne and structural engineer James J. Mallett of Pensacola, Florida to do the evaluation.

"What they found was pretty scary," Angela related.

Unless structural problems were corrected the buildings were headed toward collapse, although engineers were not certain exactly when that might happen. The original architect had designed larger units on the top two floors by moving walls off of load bearing columns, spacing them out onto unsupported floor slabs. That might have been ok, except that the builder had used far heavier concrete block for the unsupported walls instead of lighter, stud and Sheetrock construction.

With the problem identified, the next question for Browne and Mallett was whether the reconstruction could be done economically. That is, without completely dismantling roofs and top two floors of the main buildings which were linked together by a breezeway. Fortunately for Silver Dunes owners, the two professionals came up with an ingenious idea that would save a great deal of time and money.

The Silver Dunes board of directors appointed the firm MCDR of Memphis as contract manager and Phoenix Coatings of Pensacola as the principal contractor.

"This is an extremely unusual project," says Tom Ferguson, project engineer. "As far as we know it's never been tried before." Ten holes were drilled down through the roof slab, inside the misplaced concrete block walls, and through both floor slabs of the top two floors. "The drilling was really the critical thing," says Ferguson, "our aim down through three slabs and two eight foot walls had to be near perfect. It was very slow, painstaking work." During months of preparation, four 48" deep steel trusses were designed and built. Installed, the trusses span the entire width of the buildings. Specially manufactured steel bolts, 1 3/8 inches in diameter and approximately 18' long, were inserted into the holes with steel plates attached under concrete slabs at the 4th and 5th floors. Ten were installed, 4 on the west building and 6 on the east. The bolts passed up through the bottom beam of the trusses and were capped off with another steel plate and a nut.

"It took a big pipe wrench with a long bar on it to tighten the screws," Ferguson says. The idea was to gradually tighten the screws, slowly, carefully transferring the weight of the unsupported walls to the trusses which pass it on to load bearing walls of the buildings. "It's amazing what you can do with the threads of screws. They magnify force tremendously, allowing us to raise concrete slabs and walls." Destin building officials, along with Ferguson, were on site for the tightening of the screws, the raising of the building sections.

"The danger," Ferguson explained, "was pinching up the concrete slabs too high." The lifting process was not able to bring the slabs completely back to their original positions. "Concrete is not quite that forgiving," Ferguson said. Although, in some spots slabs had sagged as much as 2 ½ ", the tightening of the screws was able to bring them up as high as 1 1/8". "That's enough to make it virtually unnoticeable in the floors and ceilings," says Ferguson, "but the main thing is that the building is now safe and secure again."

In addition, workers dismantled the concrete block walls of storage rooms on five balconies and replaced them with light-gauge metal stud and Sheetrock construction, immediately eliminating a ton of weight at each location. "That, alone, let the slabs ease up ½ inch," said Ferguson. Sheetrock surfaces were then stuccoed to match the building exterior.

"Another major problem the engineers found," continued Ferguson, "was that the high-rise structures were built on footings instead of pilings, letting the buildings settle into sandy soil. We're working to stop the settling by injecting additional support under the west side building." Yates Construction Company of Mobile, Alabama is scheduled to begin work in the near future to rebuild two low-rise buildings which were destroyed during Hurricane Opal.

In addition to structural renovation, Silver Dunes is getting a new look. A new sloping roof of standing-seam metal will hide the huge trusses, modernize the buildings, and provide better weather protection. Hand-rails along upper floor walkways will be replaced with taller ones which meet current construction codes, and all of the buildings will be painted and waterproofed.

"The great thing about this renovation technique," says General Manager Angela Rogers, "is how little affect it's had on the inside of condo units. There's very little mess to clean up before people can move back in."

According to Rogers, only one unit on the top floors was occupied by a live-in family. "We hated to move them," she says, "but it was necessary for their safety and convenience."

Other top floor units were taken off the rental program during the reconstruction, while the bottom three floors were filled, as usual, with Snowbirds. On the day workers were tightening screws, lifting the building back into position, all occupants had to evacuated for safety's sake. "We turned it into a fun thing," Angela Rogers laughs, "and gave a barbecue picnic outside."

"The total for all reconstruction," Rogers says, "has cost owners about $500,000, but the process has gone faster, with far less inconvenience and expense than we feared at first. The good news is that we'll have a beautiful, like new, facility with increased property values. All in all, it's turned out to be very exciting."

DIGGING FOR GOLD
IN CALIFORNIA...AGAIN

In four years as general manager of Century Park Place Condominium in Los Angeles, Cassie Schmidt grew increasingly concerned about the high cost of watering lawns and shrubbery.

Century Park Place is a large facility with 416 unit's, six buildings, and extensive lawn and foliage areas in the interior and exterior of each building.

Even more disturbing to Cassie, irrigation water is billed as a sewage expense along with billings for potable water. As managers and home owners, we all know the pain of paying sewage costs for city or county irrigation water that never goes in the sewer.

When Cassie spotted information outlining a way to reduce irrigation water usage and end the unfair billing of irrigation water as a sewage expense she quickly brought it to the attention of Dr. Spencer Koerner, Century Park's board chairman.

As it turned out, Dr. Koerner had spotted the same information and immediately assigned Cassie to research the idea and frame a recommendation for the Board.

Cassie found Earth Laboratory/AquAudit of Costa Mesa, California, one of a new breed of firms specializing in the reduction of irrigation water use and expense. Bob Baier and Jeff Higbee of the consulting firm recommended that Century Park's board of directors authorize a water use analysis based on the following four parameters.

1. Research: Determine the amount of irrigation water currently used. Provide proof needed to capture rebates for non-sewer usage since the water comes off a common system. Identify the minimum water amount needed to keep Century Park lush and green.

2. System planning: Design an individualized, computer man-

aged, irrigation system and management style using the mini-mum amount of irrigation water.

3. Budget: Determine overall consulting and capital costs to design and install the new irrigation system. Determine the amount of rebates anticipated. Forecast the monthly water bill reductions that might be expected on a continuing basis.

4. Return on investment: Project estimated savings over time as a comparison with the cost of consulting, design, and instal-lation of the new system.

Century Parks's new irrigation system is now installed and ready to go on-line. "I'm truly blessed," says Cassie Schmidt, "to have a president and board of directors made up of business and professional people who readily understand that you must spend money to make money.

"Actually," she continues, "the $60,000 in consulting and in-stallation costs are a relatively small part of our $2,500,000 an-nual association budget, especially in light of the fact that we'll get $26,000 in installation rebates from the City of Los Angeles Water Department." The City participates in program funding to encourage lower overall water usage in the Los Angeles area.

"Another good thing, as far as continuity is concerned," Cassie added, "is that our regular landscape contractor won the bid to install the new irrigation equipment."

"This program is almost like digging for gold," Bob Baier says, "our experience is that most users of the new technology save 20% to 30% on their current water bill, and some projects have saved 40% to 50%. Those with annual water bills over $100,000," Baier continues, "normally get a total return on their investment in 3 to 5 years with a good management program."

"Century Park," says Jeff Higbee, "should save about 30% on their current water bill in addition to the City of Los Angeles funding and sewer rate adjustment. That will mean a total re-turn of about $110,000 in the first year alone."

"To be budget-safe," adds Cassie Schmidt, "we're projecting a bit lower at $30,000 to $50,000 first year savings. If we reach the top of that lower estimate we'll cover our installation costs in the first year. After that," she laughs, "the savings go on year after year."

Recent experience of the Bel-Air Crest Master Condominium Association in Los Angeles provides solid verification of Century Park's anticipated success. Rick and Fiona Cole, managers of Bel-Air Crest, have installed the new irrigation management technology at the direction of the Bel-Air Crest Board of Directors. "In the first six month's operation of our new irrigation equipment and water management system," Fiona Cole reports, "we're achieving a 46% water use reduction."

ASSOCIATION LOWERS PAST DUE
ASSESSMENTS 40% IN 7 MONTHS!

We've all groaned at the horror stories of association members who abuse and disrupt managers and boards to the extent that management, finances, owner relationships, often properties themselves, become shambles. This report is a wonderful mirror image...one of board members who took office, then searched for and found a soundly effective management firm and a manager to match.

They set about harmonizing so well with new management that crucial gains were made in the stability and financial condition of their association as well as a much needed property improvement. When asked to comment about their success, board members Joan Zamora, vice president, David Corpus, treasurer, Marla Bautista, secretary, and member at large, Ralph Solis, through president Jim Okleshon soundly commended manager David Dubin.

"David is an excellent manager and a fine young man," president Jim Okleshon expounded. "He and his company have quickly made important contributions to our association in the few months they've been on board."

"I was born in Philadelphia, Pennsylvania," Dubin says, "on tax day 1968, the youngest of six children. But my family came to Glendale when I was 6 so I've really spent most of my life in California." Married four years, he and his wife have no children as yet. Dubin moved into a career in property management just after graduation from California State University - Northridge, when he was offered employment by Sandy Brzezinski and Bob Berthold, principals of HOA Management Professionals, Inc.

"They took a freshly educated young graduate," Dubin says, "and honed him into the management professional I consider myself to be today."

"In a certain way," Dubin continues, "California Glen is unique compared to most condominium communities." The 238 unit project was designed entirely as individual detached homes, each with it's own connected garage, limited but well manicured lawn space, shrubs, shade trees, and palms. The five home models are spacious, varying from about 1800 to 2100 square feet of living space, finished in a variety of fashionable, tropical pastels. The property is located in the city of Lakeview Terrace, like Dubin's hometown of Glendale, a suberb of Los Angeles.

The first advantage of David Dubin's connection came to the California Glen Association quickly. "HOA Management operates a bit differently from many other companies," Dubin explains, "so from the start the board saved substantially in management fees."

Equally important, from the beginning of his assignment in October 1997 Dubin, under the board's direction, aggressively pursued a major problem with assessment delinquencies. Unpaid assessments had piled up to over $100,000, a revenue shortage large enough to cripple the average association's finances.

"No one likes to take a tough stance with fellow association members," Dubin relates, "but the board stood firm because it was so important to the future of the property." Filings in Municipal Small Claims Court along with non-judicial procedures such as mechanics liens and foreclosures were handled out of California Glen's onsite management office. "It has proven effective in bringing down delinquencies," Dubin says, "and being able to handle it right out of our office has saved us a lot of money in legal fees. As of May 29,1998 our delinquencies were down close to $60,000, about a 40 % drop in 7 months."

A vital goal set and achieved was to improve California Glen's records system and it's methods used for keeping members continuously informed. Dubin sends a complete, approved copy of minutes of the board of directors meeting to every homeowner each month. "Not only does it keep everyone fully aware of what's going on," he says, "but it's a great, inexpensive way to send important notices and announcements.

"A similar system prepares board members for their monthly meeting. "We mail a monthly management report to each board member a week before the meeting," Dubin says, "so they have plenty of time to review the information." The management report then becomes the agenda for the board meeting. "It works really well," Dubin continues, "and board members seem to find it easy to follow the information flow throughout the meeting."

"Together, we tackled another thorny problem," Dubin relates. The California Glen Association had been embroiled for several years in pending legal action with the original developer over a construction defect. "After a good bit of study and discussion," Dubin says, "the board agreed that it was more advantageous to accept a reasonable settlement than to continue with what was obviously going to be lengthy and involved litigation."

With the substantial settlement received, Dubin, with full support of the board, was able to immediately begin a sorely needed and expensive replacement of perimeter fencing with no increase in dues or special assessments. In addition to that "win-win" situation, the fence height was increased by 2' to meet current restrictions and provide additional privacy and security for homeowners.

Another major project already on Dubin's agenda is the resurfacing of the 14 streets on California Glen property. Some areas of the 10 year old streets can be simply resealed Durbin explained. However, a substantial portion of the paving will have to be removed with skimming machines and the upper strata completely repaved, at a total cost of $75,000. "This project," Durbin comments, "really points up the great benefit of having thorough, carefully engineered reserve studies and the establishment of specific financial reserves. Past California Glen boards planned far ahead for this repair and the money we'll need is already in the bank."

"Perhaps the greatest advantage for all of us," says Dubin, "is the kind of relationship we're blessed to have. This board is just great. They interact so well together without being aggressive, condescending or demanding. They are so very polite, and carefully follow Robert's Rules of Order to make meetings highly efficient and professional."

"In an unusual way," Dubin concludes, "I've come full circle with California Glen." It turns out that David Dubin's brother, Billy Dubin and his wife Susan, are original owners at California Glen, having bought a unit during the initial construction phase. "That," says Dubin, "afforded me the opportunity to see the whole complex built from the ground up. I feel I really know the place inside and out. Now, it's great to be able to play a major role in the management and maintenance of this fine property."

A fine condominium property, supportive home owners, an

outstanding, cooperative board of directors, an efficient, effective management company to work for...!

A world of community association managers across America will tell you it doesn't get much better than that, especially at just 30 years old!

NETWORKING AND AN OPEN DOOR
EFFECT GOOD MANAGEMENT

Margaret-Mary "Mitzi" Phillips, manager of Fort Lauderdale, Florida's Runaway Bay Condominium holds more than notable status for long term service in community association management. She is also among the earliest management professionals who earned designation as a Florida Licensed Community Association Manager.

"Mitzi has been our manager for 21 years," says Gladys Tendler, "and that's quite a record." If anyone should know, it's Mrs. Tendler. She has been a resident owner for the same 21 years, and has served several stints on Runaway Bay's board of directors, recently completing a 3 year term. Currently she continues to serve closely with Mitzi Phillips as an afternoon assistant in the condo office. "I have great respect for Mitzi," Mrs. Tendler elaborates, "both as friend and manager."

Built in 1974, Runaway Bay incorporates a single, ten story, concrete structure with 93 gracious, balconied, units. As in most condominiums, unit sizes and the number of bedrooms vary, though the average 2 bedroom, 2 bath residence provides nearly 1400 square feet of living space, including balcony area. "Our corner units," Mitzi says, "have wrap around balconies giving us wide views in two directions."

Mitzi Phillips and Gladys Tendler both agree that Runaway Bay's highly accessible location and life enhancing amenities make it a great place to live. Residents have the use of a heated swimming pool, tennis court, shuffleboard, a sauna for men and another for women, fully appointed exercise facility, reading room, recreation room, and a laundry area. The condominium is, in the main, a residential facility with 89 of the 93 units occupied by permanent residents. In order to maintain that quality of residential lifestyle, the condo documents require that a unit can be rented only after two years of ownership. "We have a wonderful, congenial blend of fellow residents," Mitzi says, "people of all ages from their 20's...all the way up to retirees."

In fact, Mitzi Phillips is not only the manager at Runaway Bay, she and her husband, Gene, have owned a unit and lived there for the past ten years. "There can be a downside to that, though," Gladys Tendler chimes in. "After office hours when people have a problem, guess who they call?...Mitzi! I know it's unfair to her, but she's always there when needed."

"In these 21 years," Mitzi says, "our area of Fort Lauderdale has grown extensively. It is now quite upscale, and includes several ritzy hotels within a block or so of us." In addition, Fort Lauderdale's new Convention Center is just a few blocks away. Phillips describes Runaway Bay's central, in-town, location as a haven of convenience. "Within easy walking distance," she relates, " we have banks, grocery stores, hair dressers and barbers, a world of shopping, as well as restaurants of most every kind." Two blocks away is Fort Lauderdale's Federal Highway, the international airport is nearby, the inland Intercoastal Waterway can be seen from upper balconies, and Atlantic Ocean beaches are within two miles.

"At night," Mitzi adds, " from higher balconies we can see lighted ships coming in to the harbor at Port Everglades, as well as the lovely skyline of Fort Lauderdale. It is a beautiful, peaceful sight."

Runaway Bay is a gated community using automatic, electronically controlled gateways rather than security staff. Security is augmented with effective security lighting, and a central, video camera, security observation system. "This has recently been greatly enhanced," Mitzi cites, "with a video taping system that maintains a record of all comings and goings during times when the office is closed. It has already served us well in several incidents." Video guarded areas include the driveway entrance to the property, the front entrance and service doors, and the elevator.

Resident parking is especially convenient at Runaway Bay with one covered parking space designated for each unit, along with a second, non-covered, space.

Maintenance has been a major thrust of management concern during the 21 years of Mitzi Phillips tenure at Runaway Bay. "I've been blessed to have wonderful people on our board of directors who have understood the need to budget monies for preventive maintenance," Mitzi explains. Unlike so many South Florida condominiums, Runaway Bay has had no major structural decay due to spalling. "When we became aware that balcony carpeting was the main cause of spalling and balcony failure," Mitzi adds, "our board quickly agreed to order the carpeting removed."

The building is re-sealed, painted, and re-roofed on scheduled basis. "Our last re-roofing was really well done," Mitzi comments. "We've followed up with regular inspections and meticulous preventative maintenance, so we've only had one minor leak in 11 years."

In line with the continuing maintenance program, resealing and painting of the building is already budgeted again, with much of the $180,000 - $200,000 cost funded through pre-paid reserves. Another pending, vital, preventative maintenance project is the renovation of Runaway Bay's fire alarm system, estimated to cost $50,000.

"Mitzi has been especially effective for us," Gladys Tendler says, "in carefully reviewing utility costs. When gas and water bills mysteriously soared she brought in utility company technicians and even stayed in the office late at night until leaks in both systems were pinpointed. We received a credit on our water bill for $9,000."

Other major maintenance projects which have enhanced the living environment and controlled costs for Runaway Bay owners in recent years are the conversion to energy efficient lighting throughout common areas of the condominium; replacement of old leaky galvanized water piping with long lasting copper; resurfacing of the swimming pool, deck, and the purchase of new deck furniture; resurfacing of marble floor areas to restore their original look of elegance; new carpeting in hallways; and resealing of the parking lot including a new membrane in upper level parking above the garage.

"It's important to remember that maintenance projects in an older building often come with unexpected expense," Mitzi interjects. "In replacing that membrane we found damaged electrical conduit underneath which cost an unplanned $74,000 to correct. In line with that, understanding that our building is older, our board has specifically expanded renovation planning and budgeting over the last five years." Following that on-going format, Mitzi followed up with bids, at the board's request, for renovation of Runaway Bay's tennis and shuffleboard court surfaces and lighting.

"Two main philosophies have guided me during these wonderful years at Runaway Bay," Mitzi Phillips says. "First is for a manager to have an open door policy to maintain full communication with the needs and suggestions of all owners and to keep everyone fully informed." Extending that policy Mitzi publishes a newsletter for owners and residents every six weeks.

"The second," Mitzi adds, "is to network with other managers like myself, to share ideas as well as insight as to the quality and performance of professionals who provide services to our large building facilities." She believes that it is vital for a manager and board of directors to rely on expert opinion provided by professionals in planning and budgeting for large building maintenance or renovation projects. "I maintain friendships and regular discussion with eight or ten other managers, and that has been greatly beneficial to me and to Runaway Bay over the years."

Another factor in Mitzi's management success is that she has meticulously kept permanent record books listing all work agreements, contracts, and incidents that occur on the property. "In 21 years I've accumulated 9 of these record books, and I've found that quick, easy reference to names, costs, promises, performance, and in-house incidents has been invaluable." That's a tip all managers can use.

Though Mitzi Phillip's heart and efforts are concentrated in Runaway Bay, wider involvement in her city looms just as large. Her son-in-law, Jim Naugle, served as Fort Lauderdale's mayor for many years. Her daughter, Carol-Lisa Phillips (Naugle), Mayor Naugle's wife and first lady of the city, is a practicing attorney, recently appointed to a statewide task force by Commissioner Tom Gallagher. "In fact," Mitzi says, "Carol-Lisa and Jim Naugle first met at a Runaway Bay party."

"Now..., being a grandmother," says Mitzi, "and spending time with my three year old grand daughter, Rachel, has taken on a whole new meaning in addition to all the other things I enjoy at Runaway Bay."

GREAT RAPPORT REVITALIZES
A HOMEOWNER'S ASSOCIATION

"Tom Rader has a great knack for working with people," says Joyce Van Haren, association president of the Homeowners of Port Charlotte Village, Inc. "Even more," she explains, "he has a real flair for finding a way to do everything the board wants to accomplish."

"In seven years at Port Charlotte," Rader, the association's general manager affirms, "I've had nothing but great support and cooperation from the boards and all four presidents I've worked for."

Testament to a vital spirit of teamwork is the renewal that has taken place in recent years at Port Charlotte Village, one of South Florida's premier mobile home owners associations. It is located just across the Peace River from the city of Punta Gorda.

Incorporated as a Cooperative rather than a Condominium under Florida law, Port Charlotte owners are deeded a 1/435th portion of the entire property, equal to the total number of home sites. The land under each home is dedicated for the exclusive use and control of an owner who places his or her personally owned home on the site. Approximately 405 are owners, and members of the association, while about 30 rent sites from the association on which to station their own mobile homes.

Port Charlotte Village is a very active retirement community for seniors 55 or older, according to Van Haren, with lots of green belts and a woodsy recreation area owners refer to as 'The Pines'. Activities include horseshoes, shuffleboard courts, a pool room, picnic areas, Italian lawn bowling called Bocci Ball, a community swimming pool, and a golf driving range. "We're also planning for a golf putting green," Van Haren says.

Port Charlotte's clubhouse has been named Tanner Hall in honor of Lynn Tanner who, for years, coordinated it's many club functions such as sewing, card games, socials, line dancing, the

Charlotteers and Happy Villagers chorus groups, as well as special events like a "Nite at the Races."

Port Charlotte Village was established in the mid 70's by a developer who retained control until 15 years later when the property was sold to individual owners.

"Unfortunately, when our association took over," says Joyce Van Haren, "it was no secret that the previous owner had let the facility decline, and we really had our work 'cut out' for us to bring it back up to the standard we like."

Tom Rader began his relationship with Port Charlotte Village as Maintenance Supervisor with more than 20 years of career experience in industrial maintenance management. "We were all working hard to revitalize Port Charlotte," Joyce Van Haren explains, "and we were impressed with the energy and good sense Tom brought to a demanding job."

Owners and the 7 board members noticed another thing, too, according to Van Haren. Tom Rader really cared about every owner. He would take time to visit them personally, to discuss specific problems or questions they might have, to straighten out troubling rumors with fact.

"When the previous manager resigned," Van Haren says, "we knew Tom was the man for the job, even though a considerable amount of cross-training and preparation were required." Rader studied, tested for, and obtained his Community Association Managers license. In 1996 owners established their own Port Charlotte Village Realty company, so Rader went to real estate school and obtained his Florida real estate license. After working for the required year under the supervision of a real estate broker he again went to school and obtained his brokers license. Rader attended the Florida Mobile Home 'Manufactured Housing Educational Institute', studying three courses which lead to it's Accredited Community Manager designation. In addition he has qualified for the State Dealers License which is required to handle the sale of mobile homes, and expanded his skill in the use of computers.

"Looking back over the years we've really accomplished a lot," Rader muses. In fact, a wealth of urgent, as well as less critical renovation, projects have added to the beauty and owner enjoyment of the shared Port Charlotte Village home environment. Assessments have been adjusted to create maintenance reserves mandated by Florida law. Interest rates on the original purchase mortgage have been negotiated, lowering them twice, while paying off more than $2,500,000 of association debt.

Profits from the operation of Port Charlotte's own real estate company have contributed to debt reduction. Streets which were in very rough condition have been resurfaced. A gazebo, sidewalks, and landscaping have been added. Fences have been built, rebuilt and extended to improve visual boundaries, although Port Charlotte Village is not a gated community.

Years of negotiation brought the settlement of a new easement line giving owners access to lakes bordering one side of the property. A new "Post Office" was built with larger mail boxes. The Tanner Hall clubhouse has received a new roof, new ceilings, a card room, french doors on the pool room, new carpeting, as well as the winning of a battle with termites.

An original sewer treatment plant located on-site has been removed and municipal sewerage service established. Street lighting has been replaced and new units installed to improve night security. Drainage ditches have been cleared. A new drainage line from the pool has been installed. Two new foot bridges and two new horseshoe pits have been built by volunteers.

In fact, committee and volunteer work is a vital part of Port Charlotte success, evidenced by water pressure checks completed on all units by volunteers.

Association operating assessments have been held to a reasonable $126 monthly covering water and sewer costs, TV cable, lawn and common area landscaping maintenance, as well as management operating expenses. "In addition to the purchase price of a home," says Tom Rader, "other costs for a homeowner, other than daily living expense, are usually limited to electricity and telephone."

"We have the kind of cooperative spirit here at Port Charlotte Village," Tom Rader says, "that makes it fun to come to work every day. We simply have an open door policy, available to answer any question or help with a problem at any time."

In fact, Rader goes a step further, meeting with home owners in their homes whenever possible. "Our staff likes the family atmosphere and responds in the same way," Rader elaborates.

Port Charlotte has a 7 person staff in addition to manager Tom Rader, with Faye Powell as office manager. Following Rader's example of career study and growth, Maintenance Supervisor Carol Yagley has a degree in horticulture, and recently obtained her National Pool License, allowing pool maintenance to be done by an in-house crew rather than more costly contract work.

"An outside accounting firm handles the major part of our accounting," Rader says, "and our staffing is leased through an employee firm, but works under my direction."

"We've been glad many times over of our decision to offer Tom Rader the position of Port Charlotte Village manager," association president Joyce Van Haren concludes. "We know how lucky we are to have a great staff and a manager like Tom to take care of us. We hope they feel our appreciation every day."

HANDLING COLLECTIONS,
LIENS AND FORECLOSURES

"In recent times," says Ray Newman, "collecting unpaid community association assessments has grown more confusing as several Federal Circuit Courts have issued conflicting opinions on the handling of these debts." Newman is an attorney practicing in Northwest Florida's Fort Walton Beach/Destin area. He specializes in community association law in addition to his regular practice. He is also a member of the North Gulf Coast Chapter of the Community Associations Institute, probing the subject as keynote speaker at a recent luncheon meeting of the chapter in Destin.

"The problem," Newman continues, "is with legal interpretation of the Federal Fair Debt Collection Practices Act of 1978." Under terms of the law collectors must treat debtors fairly, certain collection practices are prohibited completely, and in a 1986 amendment attorneys were included in the definition of debt collectors.

Furthermore the Act, as written, governs only "consumer" debts. In early decisions Federal Circuit Courts ruled that community association assessments were not "consumer" debts and therefore not governed by the law. Rulings in at least two Federal Districts have changed that interpretation.

"Compliance itself can be confusing," Newman says, "lawyers obviously have to comply, but community associations, and managers employed by them, may not be governed by the law because they are the original debtors. Based on some court decisions, managers employed by management companies will likely be required to comply with the Act, but rulings are not the same in every Federal District."

"The legal confusion," Newman explains, "sharply increases the risk that a community association may unintentionally err in handling assessment collection, and be hit with a costly lawsuit." For that reason Newman recommends that his clients follow a pre-planned legal procedure, which moves methodically toward lien and foreclosure, as the safest way to collect unpaid assessments.

He suggests an easy to follow, step-by-step, procedure. "Let's assume," Newman says, "that the annual assessment is $3,600 with monthly installments of $300. The payment is due on the 1st of each month, delinquent after the 10th, and interest accrues at 18% per annum. All previous payments were made on time. However, no payments came in after June 30th, 1998. As an example, the steps, then, are as follows:"

1. June 15, '98...Notice of $300 monthly assessment due on July 1st 1998 is mailed.

2. July 11, '98...Second notice of monthly assessment is mailed including a gentle reminder. Add late fees, if any, to the installment amount.

3. July 21, '98...Third notice of monthly assessment is mailed with notice that a Claim of Lien will be filed on August 1st. Add appropriate interest to the assessment installment.

4. August 1, '98...Accelerate assessment installments for the remainder of the budget year and notify owner of the acceleration.

"The first four actions," says Newman, "can probably be handled by a manager employed by the association, however it's important to check with your local attorney to be sure.

5. August 1, '98...File Claim of Lien.

6. August 16, '98...Your attorney sends a letter to the delinquent owner with a copy of the recorded Claim of Lien notifying that foreclosure of the lien will be instituted in not less than 30 days. This letter must contain standard Fair Credit Collections Act statements and warnings. This letter should also set out the total amount due for assessments, late charges, interest, attorney's fees and expenses, including costs of preparing and recording the satisfaction of lien.

7. September 21, '98...Initiate lien foreclosure proceedings:

A. Secure copy of deed and chain of title abstract to confirm ownership and identify senior and junior lien holders.

B. Prepare, file, and serve owners and all junior lien holders with a copy of foreclosure complaint.

C. Include a claim for damages.

8. No date listed...Final judgement of foreclosure is entered. No date is listed because this date is set at the pleasure of the court.

9. No date listed...Foreclosure sale is conducted at the courthouse door. The association should bid an amount equal to it's assessments, costs, and other charges. If the association is forced to take ownership of the property it may not owe monthly mortgage payments, however, this should be previously researched and determined by your local attorney. In most, if not all, jurisdictions steps 5 through 9 must be handled by an attorney. No date is listed because this date is set at the pleasure of the court and/or the sheriff's office.

"The hoped for goal," Ray Newman concludes, "is that the owner will respond and make up the back assessments before the filing of the Claim of Lien. In far too many cases, however, the owner with several months of past due assessments has financial problems that cannot be resolved. The good thing, then, is that the procedure for lien and foreclosure has been established in a timely manner.

Note: This is a procedure discussed by a Florida attorney, within a specific time frame. It is presented here only as a point of general reference. Any owner, board member, or manager interested in these general guidelines should consult his or her association attorney for more specific, current, Federal or State Statutes.

AN 8 STEP ATTACK ON
DIRTY, SMELLY TRASH CHUTES

"Truth is, when you walk past the door of the trash chute, the odor is the first big hint,"says Phillip Conyer. "Of course," he continues, "it's a problem familiar to every manager or board member of a high rise residential facility."

Conyer should know. He's been a property manager for 25 years, presently administering the Harbor House in ritzy Bal Harbor, Florida just north of Miami Beach. Harbor House is comprised of two 15 story buildings fronting the Atlantic Ocean on one side and Florida's Inter-Coastal Waterway on the other. It's 804 units, built 35 years ago, are all dedicated to long term rentals in keeping with the classy ambience of the ocean front city.

"Recently when it was time to clean our four, 15 story, trash chutes, I found that the service company we'd been using was out of business, and that led me to Chet."

"Odor near the trash chute doors is certainly unpleasant," says Chet Ribner, manager of Miami Beach's Sani-Chute Environmental Services of Florida, Inc. "It's a sure sign your trash chutes need cleaning, but there's a lot more to it."

Odor, he explains, is a clear indication of the accumulation of grease and garbage sludge in the long, hidden areas of the chute itself. "More important to residents," Chet continues, " is that grease and garbage sludge attract roaches, flies and other vermin, as well as bacteria that can be harmful to human health." In addition, Ribner warns, grease build-up in a trash chute also poses a major fire hazard. Moreover, even if fire starts in other building areas, the grease in the chutes can act as an accelerant, shooting the fire rapidly up to topmost floors.

Ribner's company is the new Florida branch of an old-line New York City firm long experienced in the maintenance of trash chutes in high-rise buildings.

"Reaching down to clean the hidden lengths of the chutes takes special equipment with long hoses and spinning robotic heads," Ribner elaborates, "some of which is proprietary...that is, developed by our company only for our own use."

According to Ribner, proper maintenance of trash chutes should follow an 8 step process:

1. A floor to floor visual inspection to identify and correct any needed repairs or potential hazards that may exist in the chute system.

2. Building management should inform residents and staff of service dates, cautioning them to heed all warning signs and instructions posted during chute cleaning. Compactor rooms in each building must be free of trash, drains operational, and all hopper doors must remain closed during cleaning.

3. Filtration containers should be set up at the base of the chutes in trash collection rooms to capture biodegradable water and solutions. Filtered liquids will be deposited down collection room drains.

4. The trash chute system should then be saturated with an E.P.A. approved chemical which kills bacteria.

5. Chutes should next be saturated and scrubbed with de-greasing agents, enzymes, and hot water, guided at controlled speed by robotic equipment, and delivered at medium to high pressure depending on the condition of the chute. This removes caked on grease and filth.

6. After de-greasing, the chute system should receive a final rinse containing an E.P.A. approved protective chemical which will be left to dry on the chute surface.

7. Each chute door, as well as the compactor units and rollers, should be thoroughly scraped, cleaned, and de-greased to complete the cleaning process. All interior chute surfaces, doors, and the compactor units should be deodorized with a fresh, clean scent, and any remaining sludge bagged for disposal.

8. Compactor rooms, should be thoroughly cleaned and deodorized, and the entire chute system power-dusted by a licensed pest control company for roach and vermin control.

"In other words," Chet Ribner expounds, "when servicing is complete the entire chute system, doors, collection rooms, and compactor units should smell like roses." "We've got to give Chet Ribner and his company a lot of credit," says Phillip Conyer of Harbour House. "We're really happy with them. They've done the best job we've ever had. The entire chute system is very clean and fresh smelling and we have no roaches or other bugs."

"There's another aspect of the service we really like," Conyer says. Harbour House's trash chutes are inspected and maintained every three months, without additional charge, as long as a three year contract is signed for the annual major cleaning. Included is deodorizing of the chute system and compactors as well as pesticide dusting by a licensed pest control provider. "That gives us a sense of security that odors, health risks, and fire hazards are watched regularly and kept well under control."

Note: This discussion of a method for cleaning and deodorizing trash chutes involves a system operating in the State of Florida, although the company mentioned also operates in the State of New York. As with legal issues, the treatment of sanitation and fire safety concerns should be investigated in the context of the laws of your State.

HOW THESE BOARD MEMBERS
SELECTED A NEW MANAGER

Jan Hickenbottom, a specialist in interim community association management, guided the Century Hill Homeowners Association while Wally Fink, president, together with other members of the board of directors searched for a new manager. After a meticulous outreach and interview process, Mr. Fink and his fellow board members chose Gregg Lotane, who then assumed his duties as Century Hill's general manager.

Lotane, 38, originally from the Washington, D.C. area, began his career in community association management in 1984. In 14 years of experience and career development he has earned the national Community Association Institute's prestigious PCAM designation. In addition to that accomplishment he holds the CCAM designation as a certified California Community Association Manager. "I worked for 12 years in Washington, managing several different large hi-rise properties", says Gregg, "and the experience I gained there is invaluable."

Many managers and board members will find it easy to agree that the management of a large hi-rise condominium is challenging, with much heavy equipment such as circulation pumps for air conditioning and heating systems, lift pumps for potable water, pumps for sewer lift stations, multiple elevators, intricate utility delivery systems, and miles of halls, lobbies, and floors. The opportunity for a manager to develop maintenance supervision skills is enormous, along with the need to manage much larger personnel staffs, budgets, cash flows, investments, and capital reserves planning.

Century Hill Condominium is a haven of peace and gracious California living among the crowded streets and bumper-to-bumper freeways of America's international show business capital. Located in west Los Angeles near Beverly Hills and the world famous Hollywood studios of Fox and ABC, it is home to a "personality" or two as well as many corporate and professional movers and shakers who make the Los Angeles business community, and our movie and television industries, the world leaders they have become.

280 luxury homes are situated on 20 spacious, beautifully landscaped acres encompassing a mid-rise design that features three-story buildings built over underground parking garages. A large recreation room, a fully appointed gymnasium for men and another designed for women, a racquetball court, an indoor golf driving range, five jacuzzis, and five swimming pools help owners maintain personal health and relaxation. A feeling of residential privacy and security is important to upscale homeowners so Century Hill is a fully gated community with television monitoring of all boundaries and entrances.

For two years, after moving to California, Gregg managed Huntington Landmark Senior Adult Community Association in Huntington Beach. In that responsibility he was employed by Professional Community Management, Inc. based in Lake Forest, a city in the Orange County area of greater Los Angeles.

In responding to the offer from Century Hill, he chose to further his career development by leaving the structure and oversight of a large management company to assume the individual decision making and leadership that comes with service to a single association.

"I was impressed," Gregg says, "with the kind of experience and qualifications Century Hill wanted in a manager. It seemed to fit my background perfectly. Even more, I liked the board and officers of the Century Hill association. Right away, I could see they were mostly experienced business people with a very co-operative, business-like approach to things."

The board of directors has seven very active committees which handle planning for specific ongoing management responsibilities, as well as research and recommendations for major maintenance or capital improvement projects, according to Gregg.

Century Hill's new General Manager supervises a staff of 44 people. Because of the importance owners place on security, 25 of those are security personnel. Wally Fink and the board of directors have gotten their new manager's project responsibilities off to a flying start. "The board has already set up a program to do a complete review of our security department and procedures," Gregg explains, "and we're hiring an outside consultant, a security specialist, to be sure we have the best system for our homeowners."

"There were a few personnel adjustments that were needed," he continues, "in order to make our management team more productive. And along that line, the board has charged me with upgrading our office computers and phone system to improve record keeping, office procedures, and communication efficiency."

Century's Hill's board is quickly putting to good use Gregg Lotane's extensive experience in maintenance and project supervision. "We have some problems with spalling in the garage areas," Gregg says, "and the board has established a project to identify the extent of the problem and repair it."

Managers and board members along America's seacoast can readily understand the concern of fellow California owners. Spalling, the cancerous rusting of structural iron re-bar inside concrete support beams and walls, threatens the structural integrity of a building. In the high humidity of Florida's coastal regions spalling is nearly epidemic in buildings 30 years old or more. Spalling has brought about an entire new industry called "concrete restoration."

Major rework of building components, usually planned and timed through capital reserves funding, is being scheduled now by Century Hill's board of directors. "We're developing specifications for bids to replace all of our building roofs," Gregg relates, "including the roof over the recreation deck."

In the meantime, unplanned problems also arose when maintenance staffers recently discovered subterranean leaks in the lower garage areas. "We're tackling that problem, too," Gregg continues, "and the board has also assigned the relatively uncomplicated, but labor intensive, task of washing all exterior windows." Relatively uncomplicated?...other managers are left to imagine how many windows there might be in a 3 story, 280 unit complex of fine homes.

"One really exciting thing we're doing now," says Gregg, "is a complete renovation of all lobby areas. The board wants to make Century Hill even more pleasing to the eye than before, so we're hiring a professional designer to plan and supervise the project."

Gregg Lotane and his wife Denise now live near Century Hill and Los Angeles, in the city of Burbank. They have two sons, Zachary, 7, and Nathan 2 ½. "Family concerns brought me to California...to Los Angeles," Gregg says, "but the climate here is a real plus over northeastern winters."

Professional Refurbishing
Makes Elevators Like New

"We finally realized something had to be done," says Joe Giovinco, "when we totaled up 47 elevator service calls, January through March." Giovinco is Director of Maintenance for the 52 unit Illini Condominium fronting the Atlantic Ocean in Fort Lauderdale, Florida. The Illini's two 2000lb capacity elevators were originals, installed when the 17 story high rise was built.

"The old ones had served us well," Giovinco says "but after 35 years there's a point when it's just no longer economical for owners to spend money on continuing maintenance problems."

According to association president Howard Rogers, Illini's board of directors felt it best to contract with an independent specialist for a comprehensive, professional evaluation of the entire elevator system, and to design and manage a complete refurbishment and modernization.

"In other words," Giovinco says, "thorough planning by our board and president led us to Daniel L. Carey & Associates. Carey, a state certified and licensed specialist in elevator system consulting, is home based in Weston, a suburb of Fort Lauderdale.

"What we found through an in-depth evaluation of Illini's elevator system," Dan Carey explains, "were problems quite typical of a fine elevator system used heavily, every day, for 35 years."

Board members, owners, and managers concerned with the management of high rise residential buildings, are familiar with the frustrations and unease of doors that don't open or close properly, the oily smell of old machinery, creaking, clanking and shuddering as the car moves or the system strains to adjust the elevator to floor level.

"Truth is," Carey adds, "the elevator is the focus of life in any high rise building. It's appearance and feel are vital. Noise

116

and shuddering can badly slant the rider's perception of the entire building itself."

"As we moved ahead to the actual engineering of mechanical refurbishment and modernization," Carey explains, "there were a number of factors we felt were vital to give the Illini owners the best bang for their buck." Carey's design recommended that the reconstruction should include material and equipment necessary to completely replace all elevator system Controllers, Landing Systems, Door Operators, Machines, Hoist Motors, Hoist Cables, Governor Cables, and Fixtures. "Replacing all these elements seems costly," Carey says, "but any older module not replaced is a maintenance call waiting to happen in a system you thought was renovated."

Mechanical and electronic improvements recommended during the modernization procedure included a micro based Controller with tachometer feedback, upgrade to the hoistway landing systems, the dispatching system, passing gongs or chimes, a CRT monitor device, digital car electronic LED directional arrows and gongs, car and lobby LED digital position indicators with directional arrows, door edge protection, hall button stations, oil buffers, machines and motors, car and hall door equipment. Carey also recommended increasing elevator car speeds to the more contemporary 300 feet per minute.

In addition, through his Carey Cab Elevator Interior Design division, Carey drafted a completely new interior design for each elevator car, raising the ceiling of one by 12" to facilitate the moving of furniture.

"Illini Association members," says Dan Carey, "wisely agreed to spend money for one other element of modernization that is truly vital to extending the life of an elevator system." Heat, Carey warns, is the #1 cause of the deterioration of elevator machinery, so his recommended modernization plan included adding air conditioning in the elevator machinery room considering that late spring, summer, and early fall heat in South Florida is so intense. "Now that it's cool as a cucumber in there," he adds, "the new equipment should function well for a long, long time."

"Owners and board members are extremely happy with the results," says Joe Giovinco. "Everybody raves about what seems like brand new elevators, inside and out. They use Alternating Current rather than the old DC motors. The cars are faster and quieter and the doors open quicker. They're gorgeous inside and we all really like the indirect lighting and new tile on the floors. We highly recommend Dan Carey."

Costs for the complete elevator renovation and modernization program were in the ballpark of $150,000. Illini Condominium owners have set a years long precedent of not voting in favor of reserve assessments, preferring instead to be assessed on an individual project basis for major repairs.

Major Concrete Restoration
Begins With Crumbling Balconies

The hint that concrete restoration was needed began, as it so often does, with just a bit of delamination on the ceiling of the balcony below. Cracking and peeling progressed at the usual, barely noticeable, pace. The "wake-up" call came when a large portion of the ceiling suddenly fell off....even worse, exposing rebar to further, faster, salt-air corrosion.

"This has thrust us," says 16 year owner and current board member Tony Matson, "into the middle of planning for a major concrete restoration project which we hope to have completed in three or four months."

In a tale told time and again in ocean front associations with concrete restoration dilemmas, the balcony floor above the delamination was the only one carpeted. The porosity of carpet lets rain water, laden with salt from sea air, accumulate under it. The water dries, trapping an accumulation of salt which grows with each rain to high concentrations. Moisture seeps into the concrete, carrying salt with it, attacking and eroding iron rebar...crumbling balconies, walls and other concrete areas.

"We've got a big job ahead of us," Matson continues, " because, truth is, much more needs to be done." The six story, 40 unit building was sealed and water proofed about five years ago. "The timing was right to have it done," say Matson, "but we ended up with a very poor job." Unfortunately, board and management could not locate the warranty and then the contractor passed away suddenly. "We have no recourse," Tony laments, "so that work must be done again, too."

The Sand Dollar Condominium is located right on the Atlantic Ocean, in Crescent Beach, near St. Augustine, Florida. Though Crescent Beach is nearly ten miles south, residents consider it a suburb of St. Augustine which is their postal address. There are four six story buildings, one with 48 units, three with 40.

"In the early years," Tony says, "owners in the different buildings didn't seem able to manage together very well, so we separated into Sand Dollar #1, 2, 3, and 4. Each building has it's own self contained association with an individual board of directors and management." The Matson's unit is in Sand Dollar Condominium #3.

Tony Matson, now 67, and his wife Penny have been married 45 years. It was obvious from discussions during our interview that they work closely together as a team. Having overcome the effects of a stroke three years ago, Tony is serving another term on the board of directors, and Penny clearly is his compatriot in the strategy he brings to board service.

"We came here from Gainesville and moved in when the building was new," Tony relates, "one of the first families to move in." Matson served on the 5 person board of directors of Sand dollar #3 for two terms in those earlier years, one of the terms as president of the association. "Sand Dollar is a great place to live," Tony interjects, "as we speak I'm sitting here enjoying a great view of the Atlantic Ocean."

Like so many well located condominium developments, their home has been a good investment, too. "The units have nearly tripled in value," Tony says, "in the 16 years we've lived here."

As with thousands of other ocean front condo owners, keeping deadly hurricanes Andrew and Opal in mind, the Matsons maintain a continuous awareness of tropical storms.

"Our unit is on the first floor," Tony worries, " but we have an edge here at Sand Dollar. The ground floor units are 25' above the Atlantic's high tide line."

Matson came to Sand Dollar's board of directors with strong educational background and solid experience in successful business management. He was born and raised in the big Brooklyn suburb of New York City and graduated from college with a degree in education. After teaching for a number of years there, the Matsons moved to Jacksonville, Florida where Tony continued his teaching career. It was there, however, that Tony found the opportunity to buy into a group of Italian restaurants, to leave education for a number of years and shift his focus to business management.

It was in Jacksonville," Tony relates, "that we had a good experience with hurricanes." When Dora hit the Jacksonville area in 1965 the Matson's Italian restaurants were served with natural gas for cooking. "The electric power was out, of course," Tony says, "but the gas service stayed on. We put candles on the tables for light. There were very few restaurants operating, so we had long lines of people waiting to get in and several days of terrific business." In more recent years, after selling the restaurants, Matson taught school again before retiring.

The importance of association leaders having business and management experience was driven home recently in a committee meeting set up to research contractors for Sand Dollar's concrete restoration and resealing project. "We lost any benefit from an entire meeting because one committee member adamantly insisted that we had to take the lowest bidder or we'd get sued," Matson comments.

Actually, at that time, Florida community association law allowed board members to select the best service provider for a job, even though the bid may not be the very lowest. The meeting had to be adjourned and postponed until the association attorney could make that ruling. "I really don't fault the committee member," Matson says, "he was trying hard to make the best decision he could with the knowledge he had. But it certainly did delay the process."

Clearly a forward thinking group, Sand Dollar's board has already researched the new process of Cathodic Protection to extend the life of supporting rebar within concrete walls and building supports. They've received estimates of about $65,000 for Cathodic Protection treatment of Sand Dollar #3. "We think it's probably a great idea," says Matson, "and it seems clear it works to some extent in other applications." However the board of directors feels it could never find a track record proving the system works over the longer term. "In our situation, we feel it's a lot of money to spend without more solid evidence," Matson asserts. "We would consider testing it on one balcony."

A complication for the project is that some, but not all, Sand Dollar units have permanently installed hurricane shutters. "There is some thought," says Matson, "that the permanent installation of the shutters may be causing some of our concrete problems." He adds that there is a 5% discount on insurance premiums if shutters are installed, but there is doubt as to how effective they truly are. "In Hurricane Andrew," he comments, "shutters were blown and twisted off exposing windows and units to wind and rain damage anyway."

Another factor is that six unit doors are hard to open because of concrete settling. "The sills can be re-shaped, Matson says, "but the main restoration contractor will likely have to sub out that work."

Sand Dollar #3 has some reserve funds in hand for the restoration project. Reserve accounts for building sealing were originally established based on the requirements of Florida community association law. However, owners voted to fund reserve accounts at only about fifty percent, according to Matson. Monthly reserve deposits have not been updated since originally set. "We'll need an extra assessment to fully cover the cost of the restoration and sealing," Matson says, "but owners are firmly behind the project and an assessment doesn't seem to be a problem."

Since owners have both summer vacation and winter "snowbird" rentals, the timing of the construction work is also a major factor in the project. "The board is working hard," says Matson, "to avoid any interference with unit rental availability."

Tony and Penny Matson join other Sand Dollar #3 owners in high praise for fellow owner John Harrison's work in designing, planting, and maintaining a lushly beautiful 20' X 40' flower garden area. "John's good work adds so much to the enjoyment of our home," the Matsons say. "It's an example of how much cooperation and individual effort can contribute to condominium living."

Asked about his own perception of the relationship between management, board, officers, and the home owners of an association, Tony Matson's continuous good humor surfaces yet again. "I guess a lot of people think the best tool to bring to a meeting is an AK47," Matson laughs. "To tell the truth, though, here at Sand Dollar #3 we relate to each other fairly well. On the board, when we get at least three votes out of the five, the issue is settled. We just record it, and move on."

NEW SOFTWARE MAKES
CONDO ACCOUNTING EASIER

Catherine Bertozzi was, well frankly, discouraged. As the property management bookkeeper for Admirals Cove Condominium in Jupiter, Florida she'd been struggling for three years with an old computer accounting system that was, to say the least, user un-friendly.

"Honestly, I didn't like the old system at all, Bertozzi admits." The awkwardness, sluggish response, and lack of interface between account programs made it not only frustrating but more time consuming than she knew a good system should be.

On top of that her boss, Diane Phillips, General Manager of Admirals Cove's property management department was equally frustrated when vital accounting and management reports were not ready on time.

Admirals Cove is a very large, management sensitive, residential development, a small city in itself. It comprises 900 very upscale individual homes centered in 7 separate homeowner associations along the beautiful intra-coastal waterway in Jupiter.

It was more than a jolt to daily record keeping when the entire, faltering, accounting system crashed. "To be honest," says Catherine Bertozzi, "in a way, it was a relief."

But time, now, had become a critical factor. After all, accounting needs accumulate steadily, regularly, every day. "With approval from the board of directors, Diane Phillips quickly assigned me to search for new, more effective software," Bertozzi relates. "I was really glad to have a hand in finding and selecting the new system," she continues, "because I'm the one who has to learn and operate it every day."

"I made a couple of phone calls to software people I'd heard about," she relates, "and asked some bookkeeper friends in other offices to explain their software."

As it turned out, the thing Catherine Bertozzi did that really made the difference was to scan the articles and ads in several trade magazines, especially the pages of national condo management magazine, Managers Report. Thousands of management staffers do it every month, finding ways to manage their associations more effectively.

"I came across an ad for TOPS Property Management Software," Bertozzi says, "and when I glanced over the specifications, I had a hunch it might be just what we were looking for."

"Catherine was referred to our local office in Clearwater," says Richard Jenkins, Central Florida account manager for the computerized accounting system, "and when she explained their requirements I knew this software was perfect for Admirals Cove." The program, designed and marketed by Property Management Systems, Inc. of Gaithersburg, Maryland, is described as a "complete, easy to learn, fully integrated computerized accounting system using menu choices and prompts." It offers full-featured accounts receivable and accounts payable modules interfaced to a General Ledger with user-defined accounts, simple manual entries, customized reports, and budget variances and comparatives, along with check scanning capability and 8 other features. It has full payroll and employee tracking proficiency, an 11 exhibit Owner Database, and a comprehensive work order/service request module. The software, which requires just 8 Megabytes of RAM and works with five different network interfaces, comes with onsite installation and training, the capture of existing databases and technical support.

"We've had the new accounting software only a couple of months," says Bertozzi, "but already we love it. It truly is - as they say in the computer world - user friendly, so simple to use, easy to learn. I've only referred to the printed manual 5 times or so and spent no more than ten minutes on the phone with technical support."

According to Bertozzi, the software, as purchased by Admirals Cove, was priced at near $5,000, far under just one year's expense for an assistant bookkeeper who won't be needed. The price of the software, however, can be tailored to the particular needs of a community since several of it's modules are optional. An example is the work order service/ request module which was included by Admirals Cove and will become operational within the next few weeks.

"Because of it's ease of use and far greater efficiency," Bertozzi concludes, "I'm able to handle accounting functions for our 900 unit development by myself. But the greatest thing is that our property manager, Diane Phillips, gets the reports she needs to do her job...on time."

Note: This article is offered as a discussion of how important good accounting software is to effective association management...and also some tips as to how to go about achieving it. There are a number of fine companies across America which offer excellent community association accounting software. You should review and compare several of them in the context of your own association accounting needs in the course of selecting one, as did Catherine Bertozzi.

highland beach, florida

CATHODIC PROTECTION MAY ADD
LIFE TO BALCONY RESTORATION

"We're lucky our board member, Roger Dreyer, is associated with the Ohio Petroleum Institute," says Alice Hodach, manager of 10 story, 54 unit, Ocean Pines Condominium in Highland Beach, Florida . "He knew cathodic protection has been used effectively for thirty years to prevent corrosion in underground steel oil tanks." That bit of inside information, shows clearly just how much insightful board members can contribute to a community association's well being. And it also set the course for a board vote to add cathodic protection to Ocean Pines' concrete repair project scheduled to begin about March 15th.

"Board member, Herb Ladenheim, also deserves a world of credit," Hodach continues. "He and I worked together, but he spent mega-hours on the phone and in meetings doing extensive research for more than a year, especially on the cathodic protection idea for our balcony restoration.

"With full concrete repair and an impressed cathodic protection system installed on all balconies, Ocean Pines will be on the cutting edge of balcony preservation in older buildings, according to Hodach. Impressed cathodic protection maintains a low voltage electrical charge running throughout structural rebar of the balconies, and is designed to prevent steel rebar rusting within the concrete slabs. "At this time, we know of only two other condos in South Florida using it," Hodach says.

Soon after accepting the position as Ocean Pines manager, Hodach, with board approval, scheduled biannual balcony inspections which led to major repair in 1991 and less extensive work in 1996.

"It showed us we had an ongoing problem," Hodach says. Last year's inspection of the 25 year old condominium found more spalling and de-lamination, pointing to the need for general concrete restoration of the 72 balconies, averaging about 300 square feet each in size.

"Highland Beach, Florida, where Ocean Pines is located, is a small town atmosphere with very friendly people, "Hodach explains. "It's nestled between the bigger Atlantic Coast cities of Delray and Boca Raton, where lush landscape seems to mask the 'concrete jungle' stereotype of some condos."

Alice Hodach, entering her 4th year as manager of up-scale, all residential, Ocean Pines, obtained her position through the national community association management magazine Managers Report executive placement program. She's been a licensed CAM for nearly 10 years with past experience in personal property management, and owning her own business.

"I looked at being a Community Association Manager," Alice says, "to enhance my people skills and utilize knowledge and business expertise gained by running successful businesses."

"My management philosophy is to always communicate actively with board members and residents." Communication, she explains, is a two way situation in which managers must learn how to listen, adding, "As I do in my life, I make it a point to put myself in their shoes to see their point of view."

The Board of Directors at Ocean Pines, according to Hodach, is a unique and diverse blend of seven members, each either chairing or actively involved in established committees that are vital to the smooth operation of the association.

"We work as a team," Alice says proudly. "They rely on my management experience and expertise to gather information whenever there's a matter that needs to be addressed. The fact that they're respectful of the manager's position and never 'micro manage' day-to-day functions really makes our operation run smoothly and effectively."

Ocean Pines board held open informational meetings to inform all unit owners of the extent and projected costs of balcony concrete repair which will exceed $100,000. Installation of the cathodic protection system will add an additional $150,000. An additional beautification will be the laying of tile on all balcony floors. According to Hodach, start up and research costs for the project may be handled through current reserve funds, however the majority of repair costs will be require a special assessment. "Because we've kept owners so fully informed," Hodach says, "we seem to have full support for the assessment."

ASSOCIATION OPENS IT'S HEART
TO A VALUED EMPLOYEE

Dominic Romano had been feeling unusually tired, so much so he scheduled an appointment with his doctor. The medical checkup revealed a heart problem, one the doctor expected would be resolved with relatively simple angioplasty for his 60 year old patient.

On the day of that medical procedure, however, surgeons found a condition far more serious. Dominic was rushed into heart surgery for a quadruple coronary artery bypass.

What was expected to be one day in the hospital, then back to work the next, turned out to be a week in the hospital and a long 8 weeks off work, recuperating at home.

For the previous five years, Dominic Romano had been Superintendent of Maintenance for the Pelican Harbor Homeowners Association of Delray Beach, Florida. Pelican Harbor is a lovely, upscale residential development of 251 three story townhouses located on the Intra-coastal Waterway and Canal C-15 in Delray Beach's southeast quadrant. It is a master association comprising two sub-associations, Pelican Point Condominium and Captains' Walk Condominium.

Like so many American employees, Dominic's working relationship with Pelican Harbor and it's management company, JMD Property Management, provides just the standard two weeks of sick leave. For most of us, that would leave a severe financial gap in an unexpected much longer medical leave.

There were two factors, though, that were different at Pelican Harbor. One was the wise and caring leadership of association president Richard Davison and Joe Dagher, president of JMD Property Management. The other was Dominic Romano himself.

"Dominic Romano," says JMD's president Joe Dagher, "is the kind of supervisor who puts his whole heart into his work." He deeply cares, Dagher continues, not only about our condominium, but about each and every person who lives here. In a golf cart, Romano rides throughout Pelican Harbor each morning inspecting streets, facilities, entrances, and planting areas for cleanliness, seeking problems that need to be put on the work schedule.

In making those daily rounds, Romano does another thing. He takes time to talk to every resident he sees, to get to know them, to find out what they think are problem areas, to listen to their suggestions. "We count on Dominic," Dagher comments, "to have a sense of contact with some owners we seldom see in the office." And they get to know him, the way he does his job, how much he cares about the surroundings in which they live. As in most any residential areas, many of Pelican Harbor's residents walk with their doggies in the morning. Dominic Romano is always sure to have a bag of dog biscuits for them in his golf cart. "It's a little thing," Joe Dagher says, "but it's a clear example of how dedicated Dominic is to us and to his work."

Pelican Harbor president Richard Davison and Joe Dagher discussed Dominic Romano's unexpected illness. Davison had an idea. He established a committee to study the concerns of his sick leave. The committee drafted a letter to owners explaining his illness and suggesting a solution. Voluntary assessments poured into Pelican Harbor's office immediately, so much that a special fund is now set aside assuring Dominic Romano of up to 14 weeks of sick leave should he need that much for full recovery.

"It's been a wonderful experience to see the caring expressed by these fine people Dominic and I work for," Joe Dagher concludes.

"It's a fine example, too," he says, "of the old saying 'if you plant a good seed, it comes back to you many times over'."

How To Clean A
Stained, Unsightly Roof

"Our president, Catherine Straub, is always looking for ways to make our community look better," says Derril 'Bud' Dehne, Director of Maintenance for Fort Lauderdale's Pine Island Ridge Phase 'B' Condominium Association. "Mrs. Straub and the board were especially unhappy," Dehne continued, "with the dark stains on our rec room roof and pool tiles."

As managers and board members, we're all too familiar with them - nasty, stained roofs that look terrible and make the whole building look old and rundown. The problem is especially acute in warm, humid, or seaside climates where mildew and algae grow on everything.

"Many people," says Dan Pritts president of Pritts Roofing, Inc headquartered in Fort Lauderdale, Florida, "don't know their roof surfaces are not actually dirty, but infested."

Algae growing there, he points out, are alive, tiny plant life living on the roof, feeding on oils in the shingles, dust and other accumulated matter. Like other, larger, plants these forms of algae have root systems, tiny filaments used by nature to decompose and break down mountains, trees - and yes - even roofs into smaller matter to become soil.

Compare it to a tree growing near a driveway, with roots binding and breaking up concrete and asphalt paving. In a like, more microscopic, way allowing algae to grow and stain will shorten the life of your roofing system.

Heat is another vital factor. Of two cars parked in the baking sun, a white one will feel much cooler than a darker one, right? In exactly the same way, a dark, stained, roof absorbs far more of the sun's heat, not only into the roofing surface, but into your home as well. Energy experts concede that keeping a roofing surface clean and un-stained may save as much as 30% on energy costs.

Of equal concern, algae and fungus, such as mold and mildew, are the chief contaminants in "sick building" syndrome, in

130

which residents suffer allergic reactions, respiratory problems, headache and associated illnesses. Algae and fungus are among the top 10 allergy irritants, and experts say the best way to combat allergies is to keep algae and fungus as far away from your home as possible, the roof included.

Clearly, according to Dan Pritts, health, roof decay, energy savings, and aesthetics total four good reasons to maintain roof cleanliness. In fact, he illustrates, a clean roof can make as dramatic a difference as a good paint job in the curb appeal of a condo or home.

Pine Island Ridge is an imposing residential condominium comprising 3244 units in 14 phases, dating back to the early 1970's. The 4 story mid-rises of Pine Island Ridge "B", under Bud Dehne's maintenance supervision, contain 244 units. "The roofs of our 8 building complex," he says, "are under a long term maintenance agreement with Pritts Roofing." So, it was natural for Mrs. Straub and fellow board members to seek Dan Pritt's advice concerning the dingy rec room roof and pool tiles. "As it turned out," Dehne elaborates, "Pritts Roofing had recently become a national distributor for a franchised product that cleans roofing and other surfaces, then seals them with a protective coating."

"We rank Dur-A-Shield as a major advance in the protection of roofing surfaces," says Dan Pritts, "and it's important to note that they have separate versions of the product for different roofing systems such as asphalt, fiberglass, and metal." Versions of the product are also made to protect concrete, brick, and natural stone; vinyl and fiberglass siding; fiberglass boats; aluminum and steel buildings; painted surfaces; and even painted trucks and commercial vehicles.

An intriguing use of one version of the product is in protecting surfaces that suffer graffiti. The protective coating "Graffiti-Shield" makes it simple to wash off unwanted "art" left on protected surfaces by unsuspecting graffiti "scribblers." With the companion product "Graffiti-Off" the unwanted message or spray painting is removed with a soft brush and a garden hose, leaving the shield intact.

"First we spray on the cleansing agent," Dan Pritts explains. A low pressure spray of 12 gallons per minute at 1,000 psi works well, although a larger spray head will provide more rinse water at lower pressure and complete the job quicker. "We can't schedule a cleaning immediately after rain," Pritts says, "the roof or other surface must be completely dry at the outset of the process." Pritt's trained professionals start at the top of the roof slope and work down, letting the cleaner do double duty as it flows onto the stain of lower roof surfaces.

"When the surface is spotless and new-looking," Pritts says, "we spray on the protective coating." Dur-A-Shield is a transparent Polymer that bonds to the microscopic pores of the roof's surface. It is designed to resist all biological growth and dirt while dramatically re-ducing maintenance. "It makes a roof surface more reflective of the Sun's rays," Pritts adds, "helping to reduce energy bills." The Anti-Microbial technology, chemically crafted to prevent fungus, algae, mold, and mildew regrowth, is patented - and tough enough, according to Pritts - to shield the roof against most air and waterborne contaminants such as acid rain, dirt, and ultra-violet rays.

"A really great feature of the system," Pritts says,"is that the surface becomes self cleaning, since rainfall or an ordinary garden hose will keep it looking like new."

"We had them clean and protect the roof of our "Rose Room" recreational facility," Pine Islands Ridge's Bud Dehne says, "as well as the tiles on our pool deck. Board members and owners alike are delighted with the 'like new' look."

The protective coating should be pre-tested on walking surfaces," Dehne quickly adds, "because very smooth tiles or flooring can sometimes become slippery when it rains." Pine Island Ridge's pool tiles are of a grainy texture which accepts the coating safely, however Dur-A-Shield has a companion, non-slip, coating which can be applied.

President Catherine Straub and Pine Island Ridge's board members figure they'll save money in the long run by prolonging roof life, while doing away with fungus, algae, mold, mildew and frequent pressure washing.

"We weren't surprised by the offer of a seven year guarantee, " Bud Dehne concludes, "that's the way Dan Pritts has always done business."

Note: All across America, in most cities, certainly in every region, there are many service providers who effectively clean roofs. There are also a number of fine products designed to do the same thing. We just happened to know of the company discussed in this article and, appreciative of their help, have applied their expertise to describe the problems caused by dirty roofing surfaces and some methods which correct the problem. Of course, the most important aspect is to make you aware of it...we hope, in an interesting way

PREPARING FOR A HURRICANE

"The two most important things in getting ready for a hurricane," says Hank Christen, "are to put shutters on your windows, and, if you run a business, take care of your staff."

Hank should know. At the time, he was the Emergency Management Director for Northwest Florida's Okaloosa County, bulls-eyed by hurricanes Erin and Opal just two months apart.

Opal, which struck on October 4, 1995, the most powerful, destructive hurricane ever to hit Northwest Florida, left a trail of devastation in it's wake truly unimaginable to anyone who did not experience it. It was only the warning by Emergency Management personnel and timely preparation by managers that brought beachfront facilities on the Emerald Coast of Florida through such devastation with no loss of life.

For those who've seen blasting hurricane winds, the need for shutters, or broad bands of strong duct tape, to shield fragile glass needs no further explanation.

However, the worrisome balance between the needs of your employee's families and the protection of inexperienced vacationers is a heart-rending tug-of-war for association managers. Along Northwest Florida's Gulf Coast it was far more stressful because of the never-before-seen threat of Opal's 150 mph winds.

"The big problem," Christen said in a briefing for the North Gulf Coast Chapter of CAI, "is that in a condo or hotel only the regular staff knows property and guests well enough to evacuate everyone quickly, to properly shut down and secure all buildings and facilities."

Employees, paid for months or years by the association during good times, are the only ones who can save lives and property when a storm threatens. They have to be there. In a very real way, it's like war. Families have to fend for themselves until association staffers can take of care of guests and property.

Good management and effective planning can speed an evacuation, however, and get employees home in time to finalize emergency preparations for their own families.

The necessity of having experienced staffers to guide guest evacuation, the shut-down of costly mechanical equipment, the securing of multi-million dollar building units became brutally obvious to dozens of association managers in the last minute rush as hurricane Opal raced toward Northwest Florida.

Nowhere was it more clear than in one 7 story, 166 unit condo on the beachfront in Destin. There, a father in his late 70's, and his daughter, who required kidney dialysis 3 times a week, made a last minute decision to stay in their condo units during the storm. They'd told no one, in fact had agreed to evacuate.

Everyone thought they had done so. Their peril was discovered only because an alert manager, personally guiding a trained, regular staff in every phase of the evacuation and shut-down, happened to learn from one staffer, minutes before the building was abandoned, of their sudden change in plans.

As it turned out, 13 feet of raging ocean surrounded the condo during the hurricane, about 1200' of roof covering was blown off, the 22 units and the lobby on the ground floor were completely destroyed along with most of the parking lot, all fences, shrubbery, tennis courts, as well as pool and mechanical equipment. It would have been far more than a horrifying night, even if one survived, and there would have been zero help for a sudden medical problem.

"In some cases," Christen defined, "employers may need to set up a place where families, especially the children of single mothers, can be safely housed while employees are taking care of last minute hurricane preparations." It follows that a caring employer should also be sure employees have transportation and a safe shelter since they will likely be in the last wave of an evacuation.

Here are ten other criteria that are at the top of Hank Christen's list for hurricane preparedness.

1. Have a written hurricane preparation and evacuation plan. "By the way," says Christen, "local Emergency Management officials will evaluate the plan with you and make suggestions for any needed improvements."

2. Distribute the plan to all employees. "Be especially careful," he says, "to orient new employees who may not have a clue as to the damage a hurricane can do."

3. Practice the plan with staffers once a year by doing an exercise. At the beginning of the hurricane season, review it again and post it in each department.

4. Anticipate a need for emergency power. Purchase and install emergency or portable generators. Loss of electrical power is always a major problem in the hours or days after a hurricane strikes.

5. Protect computer data by multiple data backups. Duplicate backup discs should be stored at another location, off the property. Replacing computer hardware may be expensive, but it's far easier than recovering millions of bits and bytes of data, much of which may never be recovered at all. The same is true of paper records and filing cabinets. At the very least they should be moved to higher floors, but it's best to move them off the property to a more secure location.

6. Develop a relationship with out of town retailers and wholesalers, especially those selling building and mechanical repair supplies, generators, etc. In the aftermath of a major hurricane, local stores will be out of such items within hours.

7. Plan for the possibility that you may have to contract for out of town security services. Local law enforcement and security agencies will be overwhelmed. However it is fair to say that FEMA, the Federal Emergency Management Agency, flooded Florida's Emerald Coast with army troops, extra police, helicopters, patrol boats, and Marine Patrol officers. Their response was immediate, pouring into town the next morning after Hurricane Opal struck, to seal off severely damaged areas, search for victims, check for building safety, and prevent the looting of abandoned areas.

8. Develop an alternate plan for contacting evacuated employees. Have an out of town phone number that employees can report to. Set up similar arrangements for communication with out of town condo owners, and vacation guests whose reservations may be affected.

9. Maintain a high level of awareness during hurricane season. Track every storm as it moves across the ocean. As it approaches the mainland, track it's course several times a day. Hurricanes are dangerously unpredictable in their exact landfall. One day of extra time to prepare can make a great difference in the amount of property loss.

10. "With the rapid development of computer technology," Says Hank Christen, "we're moving as quickly as possible to implement a plan to put all warning information on our own Emergency Management internet website." As both Hurricanes Erin and Opal drew near, managers of beachfront condos and hotels found Emergency Management Agency phone lines jammed, with critical last minute directives completely unavailable, leaving huge numbers of guests at severe risk of uncertain evacuation decision making. Radio stations do broadcast hurricane information, but statistics usually differ wildly, making an evacuation decision even more confusing and dangerous.

Managers of large beachfront facilities on Florida's Emerald Coast, battle scarred by the devastating winds of Hurricane Opal, will tell you it's vital to set up an association of managers, interacting with local Emergency Management, to bring about better communication and planning. They'll also tell you that future hurricane preparations will be better, safer, because of Okaloosa County Emergency Management Director, Hank Christen's, hard work and caring response.

Note: At the time of this writing, Hank Christen's efforts were centered in Florida where hurricanes are the major natural disaster risk. Across the broad scope of America, however, where hurricanes may be little known, there are many other natural disaster potentials. Most, like hurricanes, are indigenous to a specific part of our country. Examples, needless to say, are tornados in the mid-west, earthquakes in California, huge forest fires in western states, river floods, and blizzards. You get the idea. The important thing is to follow a system of watchfulness, preparation, and pre-planning such as Hank describes so your handling of the tumult itself, your approach to safety and readiness, will be automatic.

Recall Fails, But, The Board
Throws in the Towel Anyway!

For several years, we've chronicled dismal tales of abuse and harassment by willful, aggressive community association members. It's been rewarding to share in the rise of a national debate on personal conduct which causes so much societal and property damage.

However, our industry has yet to find a functional solution, waiting uneasily for effective restraints to destructive management interference which, many now believe, can come only from new legislation penalizing such behavior.

According to members present, the May 1998 annual meeting of - let's call it - "Harmonius-By-The-Bay Homeowners Association was near chaos, a babble of competing voices raised in protest, demand, conflicting opinion, a mélange of motions seeming to have little tie to an agenda. Even worse, the cascade of motions had no legal meaning. There was no quorum.

It took a couple of weeks to reschedule, to seek additional proxies and attendees. With a quorum in place, the second meeting was more orderly, more fruitful, except for the most important agenda item, officers for the new year. No nominations were in hand.

In fact none of the 42 unit owners were interested in serving on the five person board for 1998 -1999. One faithful Harmonious-By-The-Bay owner, Fort Walton Beach businessman Frank Key, agreed to help. He put together a coalition, himself and four others, reluctantly agreeing to accept the burden of association and property management. The five were installed by unanimous acclaim.

The other problem haunting Harmonious-By-The-Bay was a continuing one. For several years, a majority had voted to waive reserve payments for maintenance and property preservation. Florida law and most association documents allow such waiver. Industry insiders, though, seriously question it's fairness. Owners often vote to waive reserves confident they'll sell before needed repairs, dumping the entire cost on an unsuspecting buyer.

The need for major renovations, at the 15 year old condo, located near Fort Walton Beach on Florida's Emerald Coast, had been clear for years. Despite refusal of reserve funding, owners since at least 1993, knew of major structural problems: foundation pilings settling and degrading, periodic unexplained earthquake-like shuddering of buildings, rotten and warping siding, exterior decks 6" out of line, the seawall in dire need of shoring, leaking roofs, mildew, rotting window and door trim, a defective lawn sprinkler system, dying landscape vegetation.

Another significant aspect of the May 1998 annual meetings was that Herb Harass and his son Junior (names have been changed), co-owners of one unit, were not at the meeting to offer help, advice, to serve on the board, to ask questions, even to complain about management's direction.

President Frank Key and the board quickly found that maintenance fees were inadequate to address the property's problems and at a called meeting urged owners to increase funding. By a slim majority fees were raised $19 a month, certainly not enough for major repairs, but helpful for routine maintenance and to hire experts to assess the costs of essential renovation.

Hit with the small increase Herb and Junior Harass suddenly became energized, exploding into angry dissension. The increase, less than $10 a month each for Herb and Junior, was deemed reasonable by many. Herb Harass, though, began a vicious campaign sharply criticizing the new fee, the board's voting method, the board itself, and Dee Woods, long time association and rental manager.

"There have been serious irregularities by the board and Dee Wood," Herb wrote in an open letter to owners, "and these irregularities have caused the complex to be in the condition it is now in." In truth, President Frank Key and the new board had been in office less than 3 months, facing major repair problems unfunded and growing worse for years. Nevertheless, Herb Harass stridently accused the board of "misrepresentations" of meeting minutes, "misappropriation" of association funds, "overpayments" on invoices, paying for work not done, spending without bids, of "spending that goes unchecked by Dee Woods and Frank Key."

Minutes of the May meeting were "a fabrication of actual events," he wrote homeowners, and "may have broken some Federal laws." Allegations of irregularities "are being investigated by the Department of Professional Regulations, County Criminal Investigators Unit, and Real Estate Regulatory Unit," Herb Harass charged. He rigorously hindered management, demanding myriad copies of records while accusing board members of mishandling insurance claims during Hurricanes Erin and Opal 3 years before the board took office.

The angry charges seemed clearly to point to the board and manager as guilty of mail fraud, insurance fraud, violation of State laws and condo documents, misappropriation of association funds, and dereliction of duty.

In fact, board members have never received notice of any investigation nor been questioned by any of the investigative units mentioned. Moreover, they maintain records clearly show the charges are wholly untrue or twisted opinions of the actions of past boards in catastrophic hurricane conditions.

To top the series of charges, Herb sent a letter demanding recall of the board, in office less than four months.

Despite his charge that the board did not follow condo documents, he knew little about them. His recall demand had to be returned, with a reminder that recall required owner signatures of 10% of units. Herb dredged up four like minded souls, barely reaching the five owner minimum. On recall day, though, there was no quorum. A strong majority of owners supported both manager and the board.

"The hostile recall wasn't successful," says owner and resident Jude Hein, "but it still resulted in complete upheaval. Threats and false accusations against our manager and board were reprehensible. The rumors and personal vendetta will have a continuing detrimental effect on us."

Mrs. Hein speaks with considerable authority. She's a resort software consultant for condo communities and has been a licensed association manager since 1988. Her forecasts of divisiveness were right on target.

President Frank Key and the other four board members, distracted, embarrassed, exhausted by weeks of vicious personal accusations resigned en-masse, still careful to properly transfer authority to the small group of strident critics.

"Some might feel the board abandoned the supporting majority," says Jude Hein, "but look at it from their point of view. They are fine, well-meaning people who took the job when no one else would. It was clear Herb wasn't going to stop his threats and accusations. Should an honorable person, serving for free, put up with that?" Association manager Dee Woods, long under threat of firing by Herb Harass, resigned also. The future of Harmonious-By-The-Bay was, at this writing, uncertain. Unit owners were governed by a president and board members who, for the most part, had appointed themselves. They were not elected, and from results of the recall, seem not to have majority support, according to some owners.

Worse, the association lost the stability of a long experienced, well liked manager. Dee Woods' years of performance have kept the confidence of rental owners. She continued to service most rentals, 40% of units owned. However, awkwardly, she had to handle reservations, arrivals, and departures from a new offsite office. That's a format frequently used and reasonably effective in vacation rentals. But it certainly is more efficient for owners and guests alike when handled onsite.

The new president lived 250 miles away. A post office box in a tiny rural community 35 miles from the condo suddenly was receiving monthly assessment payments. Professional, licensed pool service, landscape service, and pest control service companies had all been fired.

Herb Harass strongly suggested that the association file existing structural problems as a claim against insurance companies for damage during then recent Hurricane Georges, and condemned the old board for not pushing that idea hard enough. In the Fort Walton Beach area, Hurricane Georges brought substantial rain but virtually no high wind damage. Many owners defended the board's reluctance, pointing out that insurance fraud is a crime punishable by jail time.

A very youthful maintenance worker was given the valuable apartment previously reserved for experienced, licensed association and rental management. Owners expressed great concern as to whether he was trained and licensed to safely chlorinate the public swimming pool.

"I heard the same worry," said Jude "as to whether he was trained and licensed to safely spray insecticides in residential and publicly rented units."

Another concern was the effectiveness of grocery store insecticides owners had seen in use. Rental owners wonder whether vacation rental customers may be badgered in the enforcement of "rules." That often happens when "live-here" owners take control of associations with numerous rentals. "

It saddens me," Jude says, "to fear that people here may be bullied and intimidated unless they know the law and documents well enough to be secure in their rights."

"We've seen that abuse and harassment are terribly destructive," she continues, "it's my feeling recall is often used in an abusive manner. It should be reserved for extreme instances where assets of the association are at stake, not just the egos of owners who want to get their own way."

Perhaps the greatest uncertainty for Harmonious-By-The-Bay was the future of management and financial stability.

"Herb Harass and the new board," said Jude Hein, "seem to put cheapness far ahead of quality and experience. Management systems built up over many years have been thrown away in a few days." For instance, owners say, Herb Harass is seen driving his personal tractor and mower to trim the condo lawn. "That's certainly commendable," Jude says, "but this man owns two businesses. Is his time worth only $6 or $7 an hour? How long can he do that for free?" She asks the questions in rapid fire order. "And what about the next president? Is he or she expected to mow the lawn, too? Will anyone be willing to serve on our board under those conditions?"

"I've loved living here 'til now," Jude confides.

"Harmonius-By-The-Bay is a lovely little island secret, a quiet, secluded location on beautiful waterfront. I believe it can still be an excellent investment if we face up to our real problems, develop an honest, responsible plan to fix them, and stop blaming those who've tried to serve us well."

Reducing Hot Water
Operating Costs!

"In managing a community association," Cassie Schmidt says, "we've got to be alert for every new proposal which can lower monthly operating costs." One effective approach to finding those fresh ideas, she feels, is for managers and board members to take time to attend meetings that will keep them up-to-date on new technology.

As general manager of Century Park Place Community Association in Los Angeles, Cassie is always on the lookout for ways to control expenditures. "With that in mind," she continues, "I attended a seminar presented by the City's Department of Water and Power. Their idea was to give us tips on how to save on gas water heating costs." Here's what Cassie learned, and what she did about it.

Century Park Place's six four-story buildings comprise a total of 412 homes. Hot water is provided to the condominium residences by 12 large gas-fired boilers, 2 of them located in each building. Hot water temperatures were maintained by a thermostat setting which remained the same regardless of the time of day or hot water needs. The thermostat, of course, had to be set at a temperature high enough to satisfy peak demand.

"In the seminar, they reminded us," Cathy says, "that peak hot water demand comes in relatively narrow periods. It's easy to forget that." In early morning, everyone is cooking breakfast, running the dishwasher, shaving, showering, brushing their teeth...all at the same time.

Late in the day the same major water use activities come with the dinner meal and bedtime preparations. But in that period there may also be home maintenance and leisure time activities that heavily increase hot water use.

Lunchtime brings an up-tick, but not the high water use levels of the early morning and evening periods. "The point is," Cathy says, "there are long hours through the night, mid-morning, and mid-afternoon when hot water demand is really down, but the standard thermostat system keeps the heater blasting away, paying for a lot of hot water that's never used."

Energy consultant, Tim Krause of Energx Controls, Inc. told the seminar group of new technology which can not only bring substantial energy savings, but minimize hot water complaints, increase the life of water heaters, and decrease legal liability from scalding.

"The heart of the system," Cathy continues "is a computerized controller connected to the gas fired water heaters in our buildings. In early proposals, we hoped the two boilers in each building could share one controller," Cathy explained, "but after testing on buildings 5 and 6, we found we needed a controller and a storage tank on each boiler system."

How does the computerized controller work? "The computer senses hot water usage," says Cathy, "through a series of temperature sensors that indicate demand." Sensors are placed in the upper level of the gas-fired boiler tank, the hot water outflow line to the residential user, and in the cold line returning water from the user, through the system pump, back into the lower levels of the boiler tank. Energy is saved by raising hot water temperatures during times of high demand and lowering them during periods of low usage. By regulating water temperatures according to time and usage, re-circulation losses are reduced and heater efficiency is increased.

Moreover, the technology can minimize hot water complaints. "The computer system," Cathy explains, "is connected to a phone line. Temperature adjustments and other diagnoses can be made quickly without an on-site service call." Using Windows-based graphical reports, gas ignition failure, recirculating pump problems, gas valve failure, or hot water leaks can be spotted, and other problems can often be found simply by reviewing the reports.

"In our goal of reducing operating costs," Cathy continued, "we were told to plan for typical gas cost-savings of 25% or more. Our system is fully installed, operating well, and it seems we're on target for that."

Savings, of course, can vary depending on many factors such as units per system, cost of gas, and efficiency of equipment. However, studies show the annual return on investment for computerized hot water controller systems typically ranges from 50%

144

to 150%, representing a cost recovery of 6 months to 2 years. "Century Park's return on investment," says Cathy, "is projected to be 64% in an 18 month period. We're happy with that."

Highlighting the value of gas energy savings, the California Public Utilities Commission approved a Southern California Gas Company plan to contract for the installation of 900 water heater controllers, 45 high-efficiency centralized hot water heaters, and 19 boiler controllers over a 2 year period ending in November 1997. The contract is the first awarded under SoCalGas' Demand-Side Management Pilot Bidding Program and has as a target life-cycle energy savings of 31 million therms over 15 years. Incentives totaling $1.3 million are being paid out to customers who signed up for the installations.

Note: The professionals mentioned above are in the business of selling, or advising as to, water heating controllers. Their experience and helpful observation are used to tell the overall story of how hot water heating controllers might save money for your association. There are likely others in your region who similarly specialize. You should consider getting several quotes before making a final decision on how to proceed.

AN EFFECTIVE WAY OF
SAVING THE FOUNTAINS

Every owner, board member, and manager can easily imagine the dismay caused by the sudden discovery of severe structural problems in a hi-rise condominium that's only eight years old. The bad news came - as it often does in our business - from an alert maintenance supervisor. Cassie Schmidt, general manager of Century Park Place Condominium in the Century City area of Los Angeles, immediately went to look. Not only was a wide floor area around the fountain buckling, water was cascading down toward expensive automobiles in the parking garage below.

Century Park Place is a large condominium community with six hi-rise buildings and 416 units. It's design is for a lovely, gracious living environment with beautiful lawn and foliage areas and expansive, verdant, atriums inside each building. The elegant centerpiece of each atrium is a large, stone three-tiered fountain.

Leaks and buckling flooring, which had occurred overnight, were first found in the fountain in building #6. Cassie quickly checked the others and found the fountain in building #3 beginning to leak also. It was obvious that problems with the others were not far behind. The fountains were quickly drained to protect cars in the parking garages.

Cassie first tried to assess the fountain problem - as most of us do - by using the comparative working bid method. She asked two firms who specialize in pool and fountain repair to inspect the damage and offer bids.

In discussing the bid information with Century Park's board president Dr. Spencer Koerner, they both realized that the problem was far more complex than originally thought.

In fact, there were three especially thorny difficulties. First, the fountain was mounted on a solid concrete slab base, but the decking of the atrium around it was a substrate, surfaced with

146

an "elastomeric exposed aggregate finish" which had allowed water to intrude into the layers, buckling the floor.

Second, the wall of the large fountain basin which held the pedestal and three tiers, was not molded in one piece as most fountains are. It was pre-cast in 16 sections and assembled on-site with joints which had to be secured with sealer. "This is the reason we're having these fountain problems," Cassie says, "because they were put together in sections instead of one contiguous piece, and the joints failed."

Third, entry space was far too limited to bring in and install a new fountain basin of the proper size.

Cassie recommended that a consultant who specialized in such repair be brought in. Dr. Koerner and a wise board of directors agreed that there are times when the cost of a consultant can actually result in savings, and bring about a job that's done permanently and well.

William C. Sterling, of Construction Forensics in Vista, California accepted the consultant contract. The analysis and labor intensive Scope of Work developed by Construction Forensics might well seem - to those unfamiliar with such work - like the design for small house.

(1) Remove fountain assembly. (2) Remove existing pool coating from floor and walls. (3) Repair floor as required. (4) Rout precast wall joints 3/8" deep x full joint width. (5) Fill routed joints with Neogard #7991. (6) Provide 3" detail over routed joints with 3 coats of Pool-Gard to provide 30 dry mils...embed nylon mesh in 1st coat of Urethane to provide reinforced joint. (7) Install Polyurethane cant @ wall to floor transition to seal entire interior perimeter. (8) Apply Neogard II primer to all surfaces to receive coating - wall & floor. (9) Apply 3 base coats of Pool-Gard II to provide 36 dry mils.

Construction Forensics recommended an even more complex 20 step process to repair and resurface the buckled flooring around the fountains. It was major construction "surgery" which included removing the greenery as well as the irrigation-drainage system and soil sustaining it.

Waterproofing specialist, Delta Pacific of Huntington Beach, California won the bid to repair the fountain and floor. "Because of the labor involved it cost about $2,250 to repair each fountain," says Cassie Schmidt, "They had to remove the old pool coating with small jackhammers..., 'chippers', I think they're called." Added to that was the cost of consultation, floor repairs, and foliage replanting.

Of course, the final step - and the one which will make Century Park Place residents feel "at home" again - is the re-planting of the beautiful atrium foliage.

"One more thing," Cassie added, "remember to advise people to water test the main basin before they reinstall the fountain".

Perhaps, though, the major lesson learned here is that an alert maintenance supervisor, an experienced manager, and a knowledgeable and responsive president and board of directors cooperating well together can deal with the thorniest of problems and control even unexpected association expenses.

Costs for the fountain renovations are not budgeted as a reserve item by the Century Park Place Homeowners Association. However, they were included with a number of other construction defects in a lawsuit against the developer which resulted in a substantial settlement in favor of the Association.

California law establishes a ten year grace period for community association homeowners to discover and pursue legal recourse for construction defects.

SOLID EXPERIENCE
MAKES THE DIFFERENCE!

Most often it's a bit of extra knowledge or skill that's aimed for when a community association board seeks new management. When Elizabeth Merrill resigned to pursue new opportunities, the 100 South Doheny Condominium Association board members had to begin a search for a new manager.

Irving Mitzman, president, and Paul Kijzer, treasurer, headed up a committee to find just the right talent. Irving is well suited for his role in association leadership. He's a 25 year resident owner at 100 South Doheny Condominium and has served many years on the board of directors. When all of the outreach and interviews were completed Irving, Paul, and their fellow board members chose Joy Abbey as the new manager.

"I really wanted this management position," Joy said. "As a real estate agent I've handled the sale of several properties here, so I know the building very well. It's a beautiful place, just a delightful environment to work in. I live 5 minutes away, so I can be here very quickly if I'm needed in an emergency." Joy, who took over as general manager in early September, has enjoyed a career in real estate and property management that spans nearly twenty years. "I first worked in New York," Joy explained, "and then I came to Los Angeles ten years ago." She has managed properties with as few as eighty units and larger community associations with up to 800 homes.

100 South Doheny Condominium has 226 units in a light gray, 11 story, hi-rise building. "The entrance is simply elegant," Joy says, "with a horseshoe shaped drive leading to a lovely entry portico that's painted in a tropical pink color." It offers a large swimming pool, 4 tennis courts, a sauna, and separate men's and women's exercise rooms for residents with the active lifestyle for which California is well known. The association provides 24 hour double-guard security and the property is fully secured with state of the art video camera security supervision.

"We're located in the Beverly Hills area of Los Angeles," Joy continues, "and our residences are quite upscale, so it's not surprising that many of our homeowners are well known movie and television industry professionals such as writers, set designers, and management executives."

100 South Doheny Condominium has even been home to a few of the world famous over the years. One mentioned is one of today's leading box office movie stars, but his name will not be made public. "Here in Beverly Hills," Joy emphasizes, " we're painfully aware of the very real need well known people have for some level of privacy in their lives." Needless to say, Princess Diana's tragic death, and the suspected involvement of the "papparazzi" photographers, has given us all a greater understanding of that need.

Joy Abbey is especially well suited to appreciate the need for privacy and security in the management of community association properties. In earlier years Joy, herself, had an exciting first career as an entertainer, a dancer in the nationally famous June Taylor Dancers. Joy and the June Taylor Dancers, of course, were a vital part of the world renowned Jackie Gleason Variety Show produced in New York City. Joy chose not to go with Gleason when he moved from New York to Miami Beach with all of his television production enterprises, including the immensely popular and long running "Honeymooners" weekly television series. She remained in New York to develop other aspects of her career.

"Jackie Gleason was not only a fabulous entertainer," Joy says, "he was a wonderful man, always so thoughtful and considerate of those of us who worked with him. He was one of the most famous TV and movie stars of his time but he never lost the common touch. He never forgot his poor beginnings in New York. Even with all of his money and fame he always acted like one of us."

Solving A Need For Water!

"We got the word from the Northwest Florida Water Management District," said Bill Bradley, retired recently as long time general manager of the Holiday Isle Improvement Association in Destin, Florida.

"They gave us two years notice, but at the end of that time we couldn't use our deep wells for lawn sprinkling anymore."

Wells that serve public water systems in the Fort Walton Beach/Destin area of Northwest Florida reach down 450' to 700' into pure water of the natural Floridan Aquifer. The Aquifer lies beneath a non-permeable layer of clay so the water remains completely free of contaminates carried by surface water percolation into sandy soil at shallower depths. Heavy development with rapidly growing water use is noticeably lowering the water levels in the Aquifer, so the Water Management District moved to restrict the Floridan Aquifer to only public water system use.

"On Holiday Isle we were left with only two choices," Bradley continued, "we could replant our landscaping with natural foliage which can survive in sandy soil with long summer periods of little rain. Or we could find another water source."

Holiday Isle is a narrow, two mile long barrier peninsula separating Destin Harbor from emerald waters of the Gulf of Mexico. Like all of the Emerald Coast it has the most beautiful beaches in the world, but before development it's landscape was dry sand dunes and tough, reedy grasses which are often more brown than green.

"The homeowners on Holiday Isle, and particularly the large vacation resort condos didn't want the natural foliage," Bradley remembers. "It just can't give you the lush, green, welcoming look of landscaping with more water-needy plants and grasses."

"Luckily," Bradley says, "I'd heard that Destin Water Users had cut a deal to send clear, clean, fully treated sewage water to the big Indian Bayou golf course and residential development. I wondered if the idea might work for Holiday Isle."

Destin Water Users, Inc. is the provider of all municipal water and sewage services for the greater Destin area.

"Water," says Erik Smith, general manager of Destin Water Users, "has become a major problem in many parts of America, especially in the big cities and populous states like Florida and California." The Floridan Aquifer provides an adequate water source for the Emerald Coast, at least for now, but there is concern for the future as Aquifer draw-down continues.

"The problem has two distinct parts," Smith says, "where to get it, and then what to do with it after sewage treatment." He pointed out that the sewage systems in nearby Fort Walton Beach and huge Eglin and Hurlburt Air Force bases required the purchase of large tracts of land where the effluent is pumped and sprayed to percolate back into the soil.

"We decided to try something different," Smith continued, "considering that our treated effluent has an extra filtering system that brings the purity far higher than 99%, so close to 100% you could drink it."

In fact, one of Smith's workers unknowingly drank the water for an entire summer with no ill effects. "When Bill Bradley of Holiday Isle came to us," Smith says, "we were already sending large amounts of the treated effluent to water the golf course at Indian Bayou, so it was just a matter of designing the system, developing agreements, signing a contract and laying the pipe."

"In the Fall of 1992," Bill Bradley relates, "when we brought the treated sewage effluent to Holiday Isle there were eight really large condos using a lot of water for landscape irrigation." The condominiums were Jetty East, The Islander, Inlet Reef Club, Gulfshore, Holiday Surf & Racquet Club, The Aegean, Destin on the Gulf, and Destin Pointe Resort.

Holiday Isle Improvement Association, itself, is also a heavy user of water for the irrigation of nearly a mile of beautifully landscaped roadsides on Gulfshore Drive, the main entrance avenue. The system, using a 10 inch main pipeline carrying 65 psi of water pressure, was designed by the engineering firm of Baskerville-Donovan, Inc. Parker Mechanical Contractors, a local construction company was low bidder at $153,000. Destin Water Users guaranteed an initial allotment of 300,000 gallons a day with an increase to 500,000 as needs grew.

"We agreed to pay for the pipe and installation of the system. We worked out an agreement that the Holiday Isle Association would pay $76,500," says Bradley, "and the eight condos would each pay an equal share of the other $76,500 spread out over five years, so it was really affordable for everyone."

Laying of the 10 inch pipeline from the treatment plant, the 5,000 feet along Gulfshore Drive, and the connecting system on Holiday Isle began in early November 1992 with a maximum construction time of 90 days. The agreement with Destin Water Users specified that no charge would be made for the water until the initial payments made by the condos and Holiday Isle were amortized. It also specified that no charge would be made until all treated effluent customers were charged and that the Holiday Isle rate would be no more than the lowest rate charged anyone else.

"The system has worked great," said Jerry LaChapelle, general manager of The Islander Condo. In five years we've paid nothing but the up-front payments. The Holiday Isle roadsides and the condo landscapes are lush and green." Destin Water Users, as of this writing, is just beginning to charge for the treated effluent. The billing rate is 30 cents per thousand gallons compared to $1.30 per thousand gallons for potable water.

"The real savings are from now on, if DWU keeps the price reasonable," LaChapelle said. "If we were using potable water for landscape we'd be paying $1.30 for the water plus another $1.30 for sewer. That totals $2.60 a thousand gallons, so we're really saving $2.30 per thousand gallons."

"We knew the water was pure and safe before we committed to it," says Bobbie Cosper, general manager of The Inlet Reef Club Condominium, "but we wondered a little what other people might say. In five years we've not had a single doubt expressed. It's worked just the way it was planned."

"This has been a classic example of a win-win business deal," Bill Bradley emphasizes. "Holiday Isle and the 8 condos have plenty of irrigation water at reasonable cost. We're certainly doing our part to protect the environment by reducing usage of the Floridan Aquifer."

In fact, the idea has been so successful that hundreds of homes are clamoring to be included in it. Holiday Isle is now in the process of expanding the system to make it available to all homeowners there.

Erik Smith fully agrees. "Land in Destin has gotten very expensive. Destin Water Users didn't have to spend a million dollars to buy a spray irrigation field or thousands of feet of piping to it. All of our treated effluent water is efficiently used, recycled for use in landscape irrigation. Now, a little income from the irrigation water will help pay the costs of sewage treatment and hold down water costs for everyone."

WHO THE HECK'S MANAGING....?

"Now...when I give the maintenance men or housekeepers a job to do," she said to the manager, "I'll try to let you know as soon as I get around to it, so you'll know what's going on."

Rather charming... but soaring on an ego trip, she'd just been appointed late in the year to the board of directors of an ocean front condominium in Destin. The city is a booming vacation destination centered in the heart of America's new "Rivieria," Northwest Florida's magnificent Emerald Coast.

In the sharpest of contrasts, however, the manager's written work agreement assured that the board was a policy making body, giving him the full responsibility for day-to-day management and all staff work assignments.

Worse, the manager faced a second threat from another director who was using his elected board of directors position to demand free management services for his condo rental unit. All other fellow owners paid 28% of their rental income to the rental division. That vital service was owned and self managed by the condo association.

Adding to the tension and disorder were a half dozen other owners, off again-on again board members, who confronted the manager several times a week shouting, cursing, stridently disagreeing with manager or board decisions.

This is the classic "no win" situation that has created havoc for years, not only for the manager, but for the community association itself.

If the timid, non-professional manager accepts that individual interference by lone board members his staff employees are torn between two, and perhaps as many as eight, "bosses."

Far sooner than later, no employee knows who to take orders from. Just as surely, the aggressive ones are playing one "boss" against the other, vying for power and favoritism. If the manager refuses to go along with such disruption of the corporate chain of command, no matter how politely, he or she has instant enemies among the "bosses" on the board of directors.

The resulting confusion and lack of focus devastates management effectiveness, and brings employee instability, shoddy work, poor financial results, and higher association costs.

With it come more painful horror stories...costly decay of building structural components such as walls, balconies, and roofs, damage to common area service equipment through ineffective maintenance supervision, and the repeated firing of good managers.

The community association management study course entitled, "Management & Maintenance Agreements", speaks clearly of the vital separation of responsibilities between a corporate governing board of directors and it's professional manager. It speaks just as boldly of the dangers to the community association by destructive interference in the managment function.

Many in our industry now say that all community association board members should be required to study and pass a similar course. Many believe State Legislatures should enact a set of corporate rules based on these ideas, to be enforced by the courts, and to include effective penalties for improper interference in the corporate community association chain of command.

"Management & Maintenance Agreements," is a course offered by the Community Association Managers School, a division of Gray Systems, Inc., although several other industry educational providers offer similar ones.

"Quite often," cites the M&MA course, "the board of directors has difficulty in giving up control over the day to day operations. It is important to point out that...by delegating authority, the board is not losing it's right to administer the affairs of the association."

The primary function of a board, M&MA defines, should be in the areas of decision making and the establishment of policies. The board should not concern itself with everyday, routine management tasks. Management must have the authority to establish preventative maintenance and cleaning schedules, procure supplies and equipment, establish priorities on service requests and in general run the association's operations.

"Many times," says M&MA, "...some board members get involved in these duties because of complaints or perceived shortcomings." That is certainly true of some non-board members, too. Management of the physical operations is time consuming and tedious. "Interference," says M&MA, "will only serve to hamper schedules, create delays in routine tasks, and result in increased costs and disgruntled employees."

The association, the course points out, has two vital responsibilities to the manager in carrying out his or her duties. First, says the M&MA, is "to afford the manager an opportunity to work without unreasonable interfering," with that work. And equally important, "to conduct the association so as not to harm the manager's reputation or to make it impossible for the manager, consistent with reasonable self-respect or safety, to continue" in the management relationship.

"Obviously," continues M&MA, "this does not mean that management should have totally free reign." The management agreement and job description should spell out the manager's authority, especially including dollar amounts he or she may spend.

However, the M&MA course just as clearly points out that when the manager is allowed the freedom to work, "within the association's financial guidelines... financial risks will be kept to a minimum." "Employees," says the M&MA, " can have only one boss and one set of priorities. The manager should be the sole supervisor of those employees operating under his or her control." If the board sets up well defined job descriptions and performance standards for the manager and all employees, it can monitor it's operating staff without being involved."

"It is a well documented fact," concludes the Management & Maintenance Agreements course, "that too many bosses will only result in the loss of good employees." If the board or individual members interfere, "it can undermine management's authority and the employees will bypass management with the result being chaos. No association needs this."

www.ingramcontent.com/pod-product-compliance
Lightning Source LLC
Chambersburg PA
CBHW031936190326
41519CB00007B/561